Guide to

SUCCESSFUL REAL ESTATE INVESTING, BUYING, FINANCING, AND LEASING

Guide to Successful Real Estate Investing, Buying, Financing, and Leasing

GEORGE MAIR

Prentice-Hall, Inc.
Englewood Cliffs, N. J.

PRENTICE-HALL INTERNATIONAL, INC., *London*
PRENTICE-HALL OF AUSTRALIA, PTY. LTD., *Sydney*
PRENTICE-HALL OF CANADA, LTD., *Toronto*
PRENTICE-HALL OF INDIA PRIVATE LTD., *New Delhi*
PRENTICE-HALL OF JAPAN, INC., *Tokyo*

LIBRARY OF CONGRESS
CATALOG CARD NUMBER: 75-135755

"This publication is designed to provide accurate and authoritative
information in regard to the subject matter covered. It is sold with
the understanding that the publisher is not engaged in rendering
legal, accounting, or other professional service. If legal advice or
other expert assistance is required, the services of a competent
professional person should be sought.

. . . From the Declaration of Principles jointly adopted by a Committee of the American Bar Association and a Committee of
Publishers and Associations."

PRINTED IN THE UNITED STATES OF AMERICA
ISBN 0-13-370734-2
B & P

To my wife, who made it possible.

About the Author

George Mair is a successful real estate broker and a specialist in commercial and investment properties. In addition to his extensive experience as a consultant to financial institutions and major investors, he has handled several multimillion-dollar land transactions and has developed shopping centers, apartment houses, and housing tracts in the Southern California area. For ten years he taught courses on real estate management, appraisal, and economics at Los Angeles Valley College, and in 1959 he was awarded a Certificate in Real Estate by the University of California. His many articles have appeared in national real estate and banking magazines, including Real Estate Investor, Buildings, *and* Bank Clearing House. *Mr. Mair is also the author of the first linear programmed textbook on real estate appraisal used by colleges throughout the state of California, and he wrote the official curriculum and textbook for real estate finance used by the California Division of Real Estate*

A Word from
the Author

This is not just "another" real estate book. It is not limited to investing alone. It is a book that combines investing with three equally important aspects of real estate: how to buy at a profit; how to obtain the best financing; and how to lease property to get a high-yield income flow.

But this is not the only reason why it is unique. In it, you will also find the same sophisticated tools and techniques used by big-money real estate investors. These tools and techniques are explained in simple, nontechnical language to insure maximum understanding and use.

In the more than 20 years that I have been in the real estate business, I have been asked many legitimate and crucial questions about real estate investment. These questions have come from prospective investors in all walks of life, including the professional real estate person himself. The goal of this book is to answer the most important of these questions. For example:

- What are the eight objectives that real estate investors such as yourself have? (See Chapter 1.)
- What are the advantages and disadvantages of real estate investments? (See Chapter 2.)
- What are the ten most common mistakes that people make when buying real estate for profit? (See Chapter 3.)
- How much should you pay for a parcel of real estate? How can you accurately judge the real value of a property? How can positive leverage work for you to make more profit from less investment? (See Chapter 4.)
- What are the skills and knowledge used by the professional bargainers in order to buy at the best price? What are the disturbing influences in a real estate deal of which you should be wary? What are "straw men" and how can they help distort the true value of the property?

9

Is it better to bargain directly or through an agent? (See Chapter 5).

● How do some developers make a profit on projects that go broke? What are the advantages of a trust deed over a mortgage and vice versa? What is the lender's three-way test? (See Chapter 6.)

● When would a junior mortgage normally come into use? What are its characteristics? What about some of the ways of financing real estate without using a mortgage? What are some of the ways to get care, custody, and control of a property without buying it? (See Chapter 7.)

● What are the seven things to watch for when organizing a real estate syndicate? Which form of business organization is the best one for your syndicate? (See Chapter 8.)

● What are the things to watch for in sale leasebacks and purchase leasebacks? What are the advantages of such arrangements to both of the parties involved? What are the opportunities for leaseback deals for the moderate investor? (See Chapter 9.)

● What are the two weaknesses of using financial reports solely as the basis for making a financial commitment to real estate? What is the A-L-I-C-E method of posting the two basic financial reports? What use should be made of supplementary financial reports such as the Break-even Chart to protect your investment? What are the four types of analysis tools to determine how much profit you are really making and how hard your investment is really working for you? What is the famous du Pont system of profit analysis used in real estate? (See Chapter 10.)

● What are the factors that affect what your net yield will be on a real estate investment? (See Chapter 11.)

● How can you use simple tables to make sounder and more profitable investments? How can you become a knowledgeable analyst of income streams with the help of investment tables? (See Chapter 12.)

● What are the factors that make land value go up? How much should you pay for raw land so you can make a profit on resale? (See Chapter 13.)

● What are the things that decide whether apartment houses are a good investment or not? What should you look for in a good apartment house property? (See Chapter 14.)

● What are the 13 important things that affect the value of retail store property? Why are you always an unofficial partner of your retail store tenants? (See Chapter 15.)

● What ten things should you look for in an office building? How is office space measured for rental purposes? What is a Building Experience Exchange? (See Chapter 16.)

● What are the things that could hurt your profits in an industrial property investment? What are the things to guard against in industrial real estate? (See Chapter 17.)

- What are the eight tax and financial pluses of real estate investments? What are the five categories of real estate from a tax viewpoint? (See Chapter 18.)
- What is "depreciation" and what three forms does it take? What are the ways of measuring depreciation and how can you pick the one that will save you tax dollars? What are some of the other tax savings possible with real estate? (See Chapter 19.)
- What are the 36 important business guides to leasing real estate? (See Chapter 20.)

This is only a sampling, of course. It is my hope that this book will not only help you get the highest profit from your real estate ventures, but also enable you to evaluate the soundness of potential real estate investments and protect your profit once you have made your investment.

GEORGE MAIR

Illustrations

Table of Contents

Part I—The Principles of Real Estate Investing

Deciding What Your Investment Objective Is (25) • Various Types of Investment Objectives (26) • Increased Income (26) • Decreased Expenses (26) • Protection of Capital (26) • Tax Shelter (26) • Freedom from Work and Worry (26) • Prestige (26) • Forced Savings Program (27) • Appreciation (27) • Points to Keep in Mind (28).

Disadvantages (30) • Lack of Common Market (30) • Lack of Investment Mobility (30) • Tendency Toward Subjective Decisions (30) • High Average Capital Requirement (30) • Lack of Liquidity (30) • Advantages (30) • Inherent Stability (30) • Insurance Protection (31) • Continuous Value Increase Tendency (31) • Limited Supply of Land (31) • Saleability (31) • Constitutional Protection of Property Rights (31) • Manipulation (32) • Not Dependent on Patents, Trade Secrets, or Manufacturing Methods (32) • Can Earn Its Value Several Times (32) • Tax Shelter (32) • Points to Keep in Mind (32).

Mistake #1: Emotional Decisions (36) • Mistake #2: Rules-of-Thumb (36) • Mistake #3: Real Estate and Work (36) • Mistake #4: Not Allowing for Vacancies (37) • Mistake #5: What It Cost to Build (37) • Mistake #6: Face-to-Face Bargaining (37) • Mistake #7: The Hidden Charges Trap (37) • Mistake #8: The Lease Pitfall (38) • Mistake #9: Ignoring Highways and Zoning (38) • Mistake #10: Do-It-Yourself Investing (38) • Points to Keep in Mind (38).

Part VI—Real Estate Investments and Income Taxes

Part VII—Operating Real Estate

Guide to

SUCCESSFUL REAL ESTATE INVESTING, BUYING, FINANCING, AND LEASING

I

THE PRINCIPLES OF
REAL ESTATE INVESTING

••••1••••

Investment
Objectives

Deciding what your objective is may be the most important single thing you do before you sink hard-earned money into an investment.

It is sad to see how many people commit their financial resources to this investment or that one, without giving any thought to what they want the investment to do for them. It is as if everyone believed that each investment returned the same benefits to every investor, and those benefits were ideally suited for what each investor wanted out of his money. This is not the case.

Consider: The young man with limited capital, few responsibilities, and lots of time ahead of him hardly has the same things in mind for his portfolio that the mature man with substantial capital and fewer years left does.

The investor currently in a high tax bracket, looking forward to retirement when his ordinary income will be sharply reduced, has one thing in mind, and the man with expensive tastes and limited ordinary income has another thing in mind.

In short, the very first thing you should do *before* making *any* kind of investment is decide what you want it to do for you. What are your investment objectives? Failure to do this fundamental thing is akin to buying a suit of clothes right off the rack with your eyes closed. The size, style, color, and fabric may be totally unsuited for your particular needs.

Obviously, various investors will have different investment objectives. I will set forth the normal investor's objectives. He may have only one of these objectives, or he may have all of them, or any combination of them:

1. *Increased Income.* This will not apply to everyone, but most investors seek to increase their regular income from rents, and so on.

2. *Decreased Expenses.* This may seem repetitious with the first objective. You may think that if you increase income it's the same thing as decreasing expenses. Unfortunately, that is not necessarily true. Often an investor's tax position is such that he finds it profitable to increase his expenses and tax deductions.

3. *Protection of Capital.* Most investors want their money in some form of investment where the risk of losing their initial investment or stake is very low. It is bad for an investor not to make a reasonable profit on his investment. It is terrible if he makes no profit at all. But, it is a disaster if he loses his initial capital, too.

4. *Tax Shelter.* Because of certain aspects of the Federal Internal Revenue Code, real estate does offer the chance to save on income taxes under certain conditions. Unfortunately, real estate is more highly regarded in this respect than it deserves to be, since people have the impression that more kinds of real estate transactions will give them a lot of *tax-free* income. In fact, it doesn't. Many times what is touted as *tax-free* income is actually tax-postponed income or *partially reduced tax* income.

5. *Freedom from Work and Worry.* I will say to you right now that if your objective as an investor is freedom from work and worry, real estate is probably not the investment for you. I suggest that if you want freedom from work and worry with your investments, invest all your capital in United States Government Bonds.

6. *Prestige.* A lot of investors have prestige as their objective. It is an unfortunate objective because it often leads to bad investment decisions. Suppose I were to suggest to you that you could invest in one of two

different apartment houses. Both require the same down payment and are offered at the same price. Apartment House A is located in a slum district, and if the termites weren't holding hands it would fall down. However, Apartment House A shows a yield of 20% net on your down payment. The other one, Apartment House B, is in a good section of town; it looks nice and has all the eye-pleasing gingerbread (waterfalls, swimming pools, lovely landscaping, beautiful lights, and so on) but it only yields 12% net on your down payment. Which one would you buy? The average investor would buy Apartment House B, even though it yields less profit. Apartment House B is the one he would be proud to put his name on, even though it is not the best investment.

7. *Forced Savings Program.* Most people would like to save because they realize how important savings can be to their future. However, it is a very hard thing to make a resolution that you are going to put $25 a week aside into a savings account. Every week there will be some "emergency" for which you must use the $25. The result is that you never do follow a voluntary savings program consistently for very long. This is why the payroll deduction types of savings programs are popular. If you don't ever see the money, you never worry about saving it or spending it. By having an investment in real estate with a mortgage or trust deed on it, you are almost forced to save and build an equity in the property through regular payments on the loan. People usually go without a lot of other things before they will default on a mortgage payment. A portion of that payment reduces the principal owed and builds up equity.

8. *Appreciation.* Another important objective or hope of the average investor is that the value of his investment will go up with the passage of time. Obviously, he can hope that the value, in terms of number of dollars, will go up at least at the same rate as inflation. If it doesn't, of course, his investment will be eroded. Each passing year it will have less and less purchasing power. (This is what happens to people who keep their money in an old sock under the mattress. Each year, they still have the same number of dollars, but it will buy less and less at the grocery store.) If things work out well, the value—in number of dollars —of his investment will rise *faster* than inflation, and he will experience a *net appreciation* in value. Usually, the reason for a net appreciation taking place is an increase in demand over supply.

These are the normal objectives of the average investor. As I said, any particular investor will have at least one or two of these objectives working together. He may have even more in combination. Naturally, I have not listed the many other personal reasons why an investor may buy or sell a specific investment. That is something that will vary from person to person.

POINTS TO KEEP IN MIND

Most real estate investors seek one or more of these objectives:

- *Increased income.*
- *Decreased expenses.*
- *Protection of capital.*
- *Tax shelter.*
- *Freedom from work and worry.*
- *Prestige.*
- *Forced savings program.*
- *Appreciation.*

····2····

Advantages and Disadvantages
of Real Estate Investment

Real estate is, in my judgement, one of the best forms of investment available for many people. Yet, that doesn't mean it is absolutely without flaws. No investment is perfect for everybody. Each person must judge the best investment or best investment-mix for his own particular situation. So, you should be thoroughly familiar with the pluses and minuses of real estate as an investment.

You should then judge for yourself the suitability of real estate for your investment plans. First, let's start with a look at the minuses so that the chapter will end on a positive note.

29

Disadvantages

1. *Lack of Common Market.* Real estate lacks a common market because every single parcel of real estate is different from every other parcel. It is not like shares of stock or commodities, where every item in the lot is exactly the same as every other item.

2. *Lack of Investment Mobility.* You cannot move real estate from place to place so as to benefit from price advantages. If there is a shortage of apartments in Kansas City, you cannot move your Boston apartment house there to capitalize on that shortage.

3. *Tendency Toward Subjective Decisions.* Subjective feelings may enter into any decision—investment decision or not—but the physical nature of real estate investments makes this a big factor. Most people would rather own a property that looks attractive, even if it produces less net profit, than a run-down one that makes a big profit.

4. *High Average Capital Requirement.* As a class of investment, real estate requires more capital initially than many other kinds of investments. You can buy a Series E Savings Bond for $18.75. You can't buy much real estate for that.

5. *Lack of Liquidity.* Real estate is hard to turn into cash in a hurry. That can be a drawback for some investment situations.

Advantages

Of course, the advantages of real estate investing offset the disadvantages. As I said at the outset, real estate is, on the whole, an excellent investment for most people with many pluses not found in other investments.

1. *Inherent Stability.* Real estate has a basic soundness as an investment. This inherent stability has been demonstrated time and time again. When other investments turn out to be worthless, real estate still has value. Practically everyone has a friend or relative who has a handful of worthless stock certificates. Too often the savings of a lifetime have ended up in these worthless certificates. Yet, very few real estate deeds turn out to be worthless.

   Beyond that, you never hear of a wealthy family that doesn't have a substantial portion of its wealth in real estate. The real estate market goes up and it goes down, but real estate always has some value and it has inherent stability. This is critical if you cannot afford to lose your life savings. If you can afford to lose your savings, you don't want real estate, you want Las Vegas.

2. *Insurance Protection.* Real estate is insurable. There aren't too many investments you can make where a large part can be protected by insurance. You can't get insurance against the destruction of your stock certificates by fire. If they are destroyed by fire, you may get stock certificates replaced if you can prove you owned them and they were burned. In the case of real estate destroyed by fire, the evidence of ownership and proof of loss is relatively simple.

3. *Continuous Value Increase Tendency.* There has been a tendency in real estate for value to continue to increase. California is a good example. Southern California seems to be inhabited mostly by promoters. People as a group who live in Southern California are promoters of California real estate. They encourage their friends to come there. Years ago, the Southern Pacific Railroad was concerned because it was shipping many trainloads of produce eastward from the West Coast to St. Louis. Its trains were coming back empty, so they started a big campaign during which they sold westbound train tickets very cheaply. They wanted to get people to move to the West Coast. This filled up their trains going west. In addition, the railroad owned quite a bit of real estate in Southern California that it wanted to unload. This land was given to it by the government. The sale of this land required customers. Cheap rail fares on westbound trains attracted those customers. As people move in, land values move up.

4. *Limited Supply of Land.* Another advantage of real estate investment is that there is a *limited supply* of real estate. As a Missouri farmer friend of mine once said, "A long time ago God stopped making land, but he's still making babies." This is one of the keys to the continuous increase in real estate values. There is a constant increase in world population but there is still essentially the same amount of land available as there has been for thousands of years. This increased demand working against a limited supply means prices must go up.

The Ford Foundation made a survey of the economic status of the United States in the year 2000. One of the two great shortages that we will have is land. If you figure every square foot of the continental United States, this country will be short 50 million acres of land. In the state of California, they are urbanizing land at the rate of 300 acres per day. That rate has been going on for 20 years.

5. *Saleability.* Real estate is always saleable at some price. Maybe it's not at the price you want, but it's always saleable at some price. This is not true of particular stock certificates or certain other kinds of investments.

6. *Constitutional Protection of Property Rights.* The property rights that you have in real estate are protected by both federal and state constitutions.

7. *Manipulation.* Another advantage of real estate investments is this: they are *not* as prone to malicious manipulation as most investments. If you invest in the stock of a company, the company officials might bleed the company dry of all profit and assets before you ever find out about it. In the case of real estate investment, it is pretty hard for the manager you hire to run away to South America and take your apartment or office building with him. Also, since rents are usually due monthly, managers can rarely rob you of more than one month's rent before you are alerted to the fact that there may be trouble brewing.

8. *Not Dependent on Patents, Trade Secrets, or Manufacturing Methods.* There is a very tight security system about methods of manufacture, because many companies' whole livelihood depends upon maintaining the secrecy of a patent or formula. For example, the formula for Coca Cola syrup is only known by two men. The company keeps it that way because a financial empire depends on keeping the formula secret. Drug companies have been faced with a terrible problem concerning formula secrecy. They spend millions of dollars in research developing a particular drug. Sometimes the formula is stolen and sold. A competing company can then manufacture the same drug at a fraction of the price because it doesn't have to develop it. This is not true of real estate.

9. *Can Earn Its Value Several Times.* Real estate can pay for itself many times over. Customarily, a net ground lease will pay 7% per year net. That means the tenant, which may be an oil company, pays the taxes, the insurance, and the assessments. You get 7% of the fair market value of that property free and clear, aside from your own income tax every year. At the end of 14½ years, you have gotten the full value of that property just as if you had sold it, but you still own it. At the end of the next 14½ years, you've done that again. This has a compounding effect because the value keeps going up.

10. *Tax Shelter.* A most important advantage offered by real estate is "tax shelter." Because of the particularly favorable position that real estate enjoys under our Internal Revenue Code, it is possible to save many, many dollars on income through the ownership of real estate. This is not true of most other forms of investment.

POINTS TO KEEP IN MIND

The disadvantages of real estate investment are these:

- *Lack of a common market.*
- *Lack of investment mobility.*

- *Tendency toward subjective judgements by buyers.*
- *Relatively high investment required.*
- *Lack of liquidity.*

The advantages of real estate investment are these:

- *Inherent stability.*
- *Insurable value.*
- *Tendency toward continuous increase in value.*
- *Limited supply of land.*
- *Always saleable at some price.*
- *Property rights protected by the Constitution.*
- *Not as prone to malicious manipulation as other investments.*
- *Not dependent on trade secrets, formulas, and patents.*
- *Pays for itself many times over without fear of total loss.*
- *Provides excellent tax shelter.*

···· 3 ····

Ten Mistakes in
Buying Real Estate
for Profit

Every year thousands of people find themselves with some extra money to invest. Usually, they are looking for a place where their money can earn a profit and still be reasonably safe. Some of these people put their money into government bonds; some people buy stocks and bonds; some people just leave it in the bank; and, many others decide to invest in some income-producing real estate. These latter people buy things such as apartment houses and retail stores.

Of all the people who put their money into income-producing real estate, a certain number end up losing money. Some of them end up losing the property, too. These are the people who make some of the common mistakes of investment in real estate that we are going to talk about right now.

Mistake #1: Emotional Decisions. Do you decide to buy a property just because you like the way it looks? You want a property that will bring you a profit. Sometimes a run-down piece of property will make more profit than a beautiful building with flashing lights and lovely waterfalls. Use your head and not your heart in deciding which property you should buy. Don't be blinded by "gingerbread" extras. Decide on the basis of cold, hard fact. You are going to sink *your* money into the property. How much money will it pay you back?

Mistake #2: Rules-of-Thumb. Many investors lose their shirts in real estate because they have some favorite rule-of-thumb on which to base their decision to buy or not to buy. One of the most common is that seven times the yearly gross income is the fair market value of the property. According to this, if you take all the rent that comes in during one year and multiply that times seven, the product will tell you what the property is worth. This is one of the most ridiculous things I have ever heard. This theory implies that, if a property makes $5,000 a year in gross rents, it is worth seven times $5,000 or $35,000.

What you want to know is what the *net* income is—not the gross. You want to know how much you get after all the expenses are paid. Suppose you take this same property and make $5,000 a year in gross rents. And, suppose that, after paying taxes, utilities, insurance, rubbish collection, and so on, you find that a profit of $350 a year is left. Would you pay $35,000 just to get $350 a year back? Of course you wouldn't! But, that's what this rule-of-thumb would have you doing. The point is, forget about rules-of-thumb and all those other fancy shortcuts to nowhere. Find out how much the property earns *after all expenses are paid.* Then decide how much you'll pay for it.

Mistake #3: Real Estate and Work. Many people who buy real estate for investment do not seem to realize that owning a piece of real estate means *work.* There is work to do anytime you own real estate. Either you have to do it or you have to pay someone else to do it for you. Suppose you buy an apartment house and you put $20,000 into it. It shows a profit of $2,000 a year. This is 10% return on your investment and it sounds pretty good. However, in order for this property to make that $2,000, you have to mow the lawn; you have to take out the trash; you have to do the repair jobs around the place; and so on. In other words, you bought an apartment house *and* a job as a handyman.

If you have to pay someone else to do this work, your profit might go down to say—$1,000 a year instead of $2,000. This is a 5% return on your money, which isn't so good. You must figure what the profit is after deducting all expenses, including the cost of your own work. If you don't, you are not getting a true picture of what your money is earning.

Mistake #4: Not Allowing for Vacancies. Almost every modest-sized rental property has vacancies from time to time. You cannot assume that your rental property will be fully occupied all of the time. So, in figuring out what kind of profit your money will bring back, allow for some months when there will be no rent coming in. How much you should allow varies from property to property. You can get a good idea by seeing the records of rent collections on the property from the past few years.

Mistake #5: What It Cost to Build. Many people get trapped into bad investments because they think the cost of constructing a building has something to do with what that building is worth. This is not true. The value of a rental property is based on the profit it will make. It is not based on what it cost to build it. Otherwise, you are paying for somebody else's mistake.

Suppose there are two income properties. Both of them make a net profit of $3,000 a year. One of them cost $100,000 to build and the other one cost $25,000 to build. Which one would you buy? You would buy the one that gave you the highest profit for your investment. You would not buy the one that cost the most to build. The point, again, is that the value of income property is not what it cost to build but rather what kind of profit it makes.

Mistake #6: Face-to-Face Bargaining. A big mistake that many people make is to bargain with the seller of the property on a face-to-face basis. The vast experience of thousands of professional investors has been that the best deal can be made if buyer and seller never meet until the deal is over. Recent studies at the University of Pennsylvania confirm this. One big reason this is true is: When buyer and seller meet face-to-face, there is a great risk that something will happen or be said that will make one of them mad. At that point, the one who is mad will become unreasonable and will refuse to consider any kind of a reasonable deal. So, as a general rule, it is always best to use a go-between or agent to negotiate the deal.

Mistake #7: The Hidden Charges Trap. Many investors get hurt in real estate deals because they don't know about many of the hidden charges involved. They may make a deal based only on the down payment, price, and terms. When it comes time to close the deal, they find out they are faced with charges for escrow fees, new loan charges, penalty charges for paying off the old loan, termite inspection, title insurance, and many other costs that run up the amount of cash needed way beyond what they figured it would be. Before you close the deal, make sure that *all* the charges are spelled out in writing for you.

Mistake #8: The Lease Pitfall. When buying income property, many buyers make the mistake of thinking that having a tenant on a long lease guarantees a steady flow of rent payments coming in. A lease is only as good as the man who signs it. Legally, you can force a man to pay the rent he owes you under a lease. But, as a practical matter, suppose a man signs a 15-year lease with you and goes broke in three months. What are you going to do? Take him to court? In most counties that will take two years, and if you do win you will then have to find him to collect. So, as a realistic matter, a lease is only as good as the man behind it.

Mistake #9: Ignoring Highways and Zoning. Before you buy any property, you should check with the various city and county offices to find out about freeway routes, flood control channels, zoning restrictions on the property, airports, sewers, and the availability of needed public services. Suppose you buy a property with the idea of erecting a commercial building on it, and after you have said "good-bye" to your money, you find out that zoning laws forbid commercial use of the property. Or suppose that you buy some acreage to farm and you find out later that there is no water available. There are many, many important things of this sort that you must check out before buying—not after.

Mistake #10: Do-It-Yourself Investing. Investing money in real estate—just like any other investment—can be a tricky and involved business. Just because you may have made a lot of money doing one thing or another doesn't mean you automatically have the know-how to invest it wisely. The best thing to do is to work with a team consisting of a reliable Realtor, a sharp attorney, and a smart accountant. This team of three can make and save you more money than they will ever cost you. The most important thing to remember is to *investigate before you invest*.

POINTS TO KEEP IN MIND

The ten most common mistakes in buying real estate for profit are:
- *Emotional decisions.*
- *Rule-of-thumb decision making.*
- *Forgetting that real estate means work.*

- *Not allowing for vacancies.*
- *The what-it-cost-to-build mistake.*
- *The face-to-face bargaining mistake.*
- *The hidden charges trap.*
- *The lease pitfall.*
- *Ignoring highways and zoning.*
- *Do-it-yourself investing.*

II

BUYING
REAL ESTATE

• • • • 4 • • • •

What You Should Pay
for Real Estate

=========================

You can't make a profit if you buy too high or sell too low . This is elementary in any business and, yet, it is amazing how many people invest in real estate without having any accurate idea of what the fair market value of the property in question is.

How is it possible to be an intelligent and, more important, financially successful real estate investor if you don't know real estate values? I don't know the answer. I will admit that there seems to be some people who have an intuitive ability to judge value with almost mystical accuracy without applying any system or technique. For that reason—so that the rest of us will also have a chance at making some money—it is important that at least this one chapter be devoted to the art of real estate appraisal.

43

I warn you at the outset, you will be disappointed before you finish exploring the subject. You enter the study of real estate appraisal with the expectation of mathematical certainty. You think that you will learn how to arrive at an exact and indisputable figure, giving the precise value of a particular parcel of property. Well, you won't.

An appraisal is simply defined as, "an estimate of value." The operative word is "estimate." Ten appraisers evaluating the same piece of property on the same day, for the same purpose, will probably come up with ten different figures. Hopefully, they will be within a reasonable range of each other. Nevertheless, they will most likely all be different. So, as disappointing as it may be, never forget that an appraisal of real estate is only an *estimate* of its value.

THREE APPROACHES

There are three methods that are normally used to appraise property: comparison, cost, and income.

Comparison Approach

This simply involves matching comparable properties that have sold (which we will call comparable sales) plus or minus adjustments. That equals our estimate of value. We take a comparable sale (a property that is comparable to the one we're looking at) and we find out the price at which it sold. Then we investigate the facts behind the sale, because just the number of dollars is not sufficient. If that is all you know, you're in trouble when making an appraisal. You must look behind that dollar figure and find out the financial terms of the sale, when the sale was made, the reason the property was sold, the condition of the property at the time it was sold, and so on.

For example, a property that was sold by a man on the verge of bankruptcy and desperately in need of raising cash, would sell for one price. The same property being offered for sale by a man who doesn't really care whether he sells it or not will sell for an entirely different price. This should be pretty self-evident. By the same token, a $70,000 apartment house that sells for $2,000 down and the rest on easy installments is not going to sell for the same price as it would if you had to put $30,000 down. So, the number of dollars paid for a property is not necessarily a test of the fair market value. You must look behind the number of dollars and find the circumstances of the sale. Having done that, you would make adjustments, either plus or minus, for various factors such as the ones just discussed.

Adjustments

Adjustments are made for financing, or the location relative to the property being appraised. The comparable sale property may be ten blocks away from the property being evaluated. If the property being appraised has a location that is better, you would add the comparable sale property's selling price in an attempt to make it as much as possible like the property being appraised. If the location was worse, you would subtract from the comparable sale price.

You may also make adjustments for time. Property that sold three years ago for $70,000 probably would sell for more today just by virtue of inflation, if nothing else. How much of an adjustment one would make is a matter of judgement based on reason and fact. You might evaluate it as being worth $74,000 or $77,000. How much of an adjustment would you make for a three-year passage of time? Some will say inflation increases at the rate of 3% a year. Therefore, 3% times three years equals 9%. Another person would say three years ago it went at the rate of 4% and last year it went at the rate of 2⅜%. Still others would use the Bureau of Labor Statistics Cost of Living Index and come up with a different valuation. It may be within a fairly close range, running from $74,000 to as much as $80,000.

Making these adjustments and comparisons gives you an idea of what that property in question should sell for today. That is the essence of the comparison approach to value.

Cost Approach

The second method is the cost approach. This simply consists of adding the land to the depreciated improvements and that equals your estimate of value. Estimating the value of depreciated improvements is very simple—measure the improvements. For example, you measure up the apartment house and you find there are 40,000 square feet. Check and see what it would cost to build that 40,000 square feet. For that information you can consult three or four different kinds of building cost estimating books, such as *Marshall Stevens*, or *National Estimator*, or others found in any good library. Another way is to go out and talk to some builders, asking them for an estimate of what it costs to erect an apartment building. Suppose you estimate the 40,000 square feet at $9 a square foot. That would come out to $360,000, which is what it would cost to build new.

If the apartment building happens to be five years old, you then must depreciate it. There are various ways. The simplest way, for example, is to say the apartment house has a life of 25 years, and it is going to depreciate the same amount each year. If it has a life of 25 years, you would depreciate it 1/25th or 4% (of its cost new) each year. Since the building in this example is five years old, you take off 20%. Twenty per cent of $360,000 is $72,000. Thus, $288,000 is the depreciated value of the improvements. To this you must add the land value.

Land Value

You arrive at the land value by using the comparison approach. First consider what a lot such as the one being evaluated would go for in this neighborhood today. Then go around and check comparable sales; make plus or minus adjustments; and come up with an estimated value on the land. If you have 40,000 square feet in the apartment building, chances are the lot is at least 30,000 square feet. Suppose you find out that the land in the area is selling for $3 a square foot. This results in a land value of $90,000. Add this to the value of the depreciated improvement and you have a total valuation of $378,000.

Notice that you only depreciated the improvements and not the land. The Internal Revenue Service and general accounting practice says that you can't depreciate land.

Before considering the income approach, let's find out where these first two approaches are mainly used. The comparison approach is usu- ally best used in the case of single family dwellings, raw land, or vacant land. The cost approach is the preferred method in the case of properties that are not for investment, or income, and are not usually bought and sold. Examples would be public buildings and quasi-public buildings; such as, railroad stations, schools, hospitals, and churches. If you tried to use the comparison approach for a church or a railroad station, you probably wouldn't find many comparable sales. That's why the cost ap- proach is most generally used on this type of property.

Income Approach

The income approach is the method you will be most involved with because it is primarily concerned with investment or income property. The income approach has several variations but the most accepted way of computing it is this: Take the annual net income and divide it by whatever rate of interest is necessary to attract money to this kind of investment. The result is the estimate of value.

For example, consider an apartment building that yields $6,500 net income per year. What kind of rate of return would you want on the apartment house? What kind of return would it take to attract your money—perhaps 10%? Therefore, if the apartment house nets $6,500 a year and you want a 10% return on your money, you shouldn't pay more than $65,000.

Other Not-So-Good Approaches

You will hear a lot of clever ways to figure the value of income property, such as using the "magic multiplier." It works like this: seven times the *gross* income is the fair price. Does that confuse you? Every professional investor shares your confusion because he doesn't care what the *gross* income is on an investment. All he really cares about is the *net* income.

Consider two identical properties, both selling for seven times the gross, but one is netting $4,000 a year and the other is netting $6,000 a year. According to seven times the gross income method, you ought to pay the same price for either one of them. This is absurd.

Another technique is to use the assessed value, which is the value the assessor puts on the property. You go down to the county assessor's office and look up the assessed value, then multiply it by four if all the property in the county is assessed at 25% of its value. Actually, a recent study by the American Institute of Real Estate Appraisers of the assessment rates in one state showed that the average assessment rate (the average percentage of market value at which the property is assessed) was about 19.3%, even though it was supposed to be 25%. In other words, assessment rates are either more or less than they're supposed to be. So, this technique is also absurd.

Back to the Income Approach

This is really the soundest approach. What you're doing when you buy income property is buying a stream of income. Sometimes with income property, investors don't even look at the premises before they buy. That may sound sort of odd, but, for example, the senior vice-president of most banks could be classified as a reasonably prudent investor. You can take a lease signed by some major oil corporation and ask him, "What will you loan me on it?" He'll say, "I'll discount this for you right now at 7%. I don't have to see the property. I don't even care if there's a station there because I've got a bona fide lease." Of course, he is going to check with Standard Oil or whoever the tenant is, to see if it is a bona fide lease. He is less interested in the property than he is in the written promise of Standard Oil to pay "X" dollars per month for the next 15 or 20 years. If they want to pay it without having a station there, that is their business. All the banker cares about is the stable income stream. Smart investors have the same attitude.

The Annual Net Income

Basic to using the income approach is calculating the annual net income. Annual net income is the end result or so-called "bottom-line" of what is called the "capital setup." A capital setup is a statement which explains what the income from the property is, what the expenses are, and what the net result is.

Actual vs. Scheduled Income

The first thing to watch for in analyzing income is *actual income* vs. *scheduled income*. "Scheduled income" means what the seller or the broker *thinks* the property ought to rent for. "Actual income" is what the property *does* rent for on the open market. For example, you may find a 40-unit apartment building with all apartments the same. You may find that 15 are *actually* rented for $95 a month but the 25 that are vacant are *scheduled* on the books at $125. This is an example of why you must be concerned with finding out the *actual* income.

Check the Leases

There are various ways of doing this. In a good commercial investment, leases are important. Check and read them over carefully. Your offer to buy should be contingent upon your right to review all the leases and get certified copies before the deal is closed. If you are not satisfied that the leases conform with the representations made as to what the rents are, the deal should be off.

Talk to the Tenants

Another very effective way is to talk to the tenants. You may not be allowed to do that until you are in escrow, but do it. Talking to the tenants is very important. You may find out that they are paying $125 a month but only ten months of the year. On the other hand, they might be paying $125 a month, but moved in with eight months' free rent. There's nothing wrong with these things. In today's market, concessions are constantly being made to merchandise space and get tenants signed on a lease. Just don't be misled into thinking you're getting $125 for 12 months in the year.

Also, it might be interesting to find out what, if any, relationship exists between the tenants and the builder or the seller. Too frequently you will find nephews, uncles, and mothers-in-law living in the building. As soon as escrow closes, the whole place is vacant. Too late, you wonder "What happened to everybody?"

Adjusted Gross Income

You get what is called "adjusted gross income" by taking the property's actual gross income minus a vacancy and collection loss. There are rare times when you would not allow for vacancy. If you have a firm, noncancellable lease with a very solid tenant, a vacancy allowance is probably not necessary. On the other hand, if you have average, run-of-the-mill kinds of tenants, you'd better allow for some vacancies. Do this even if the building is 100% occupied at the time you buy. What is true today is not necessarily going to be true all year or all of the next five years. There should also be an allowance for collection losses. These are caused by such things as the fellow who moves out owing you rent. Most property owners are inclined to be good guys and not pursue these deadbeats. That means having some collection losses.

Gross actual income minus allowances for vacancy and collection losses equals adjusted gross income.

Expenses

From adjusted gross income you now have to deduct expenses. These fall into three categories. There are those expenses called "operating expenses;" those termed "repair and maintenance expenses;" and, those known as "fixed expenses."

Let me just identify what you would generally put in each of these three categories.

Operating Expenses

Operating expenses are those expenses necessary for the daily running of the property. These are usually proportional to the level of occupancy. If the building is 100% occupied, the operating expenses will be at their highest. If the building is vacant, the operating expenses will be at their lowest. In other words, they fluctuate in response to the number of tenants you have to service. They include such things as janitor service, window washing, management, rubbish collection, and taking care of the yard. These are things that are necessary from day to day to keep the building going. Greater detail on this and the other categories can be found in Service Bulletin No. 24 of the National Association of Building Owners and Managers at 134 South La Salle Street, Chicago, Illinois.

Repair and Maintenance Expenses

These expenses are not regular expenses. They are expenses which are occasionally necessary to keep the building in habitable and workable condition; things such as replacing a malfunctioning hot water heater, repairing a leaky roof, or repainting after a tenant moves out.

Fixed Expenses

The last category of expenses are those that are generally stable for a year or so at a time. They don't vary with the number of tenants you have in the building. Included are such things as real estate taxes, insurance and assessments, and interest payments on the mortgage. For example, it wouldn't make any difference if the building is empty or full, you're still going to have to pay the taxes.

You total all the expenses and subtract that total from the adjusted gross income. This gives you what is called "net income before depreciation and debt service."

The Kinds of Net Income

This brings up my next topic—the kinds of net income. There are all kinds of "net income." So, when discussing "net," what kind of net is being talked about? Are you talking about net after all expenses but before depreciation? (Depreciation is a noncash bookkeeping charge until you sell the property.) Is it net before you pay the interest on the mortgage? Is it net after depreciation? Is it net before depreciation, or is it net after all charges? The point being that there are many kinds of "nets." The kind you will use most frequently is the net before depreciation and debt service. This is the net return you would get on the investment if there was no mortgage on the property.

Net Before Depreciation and Debt Service

When figuring whether you should invest in this property or not, you want to see what the property would pay on its asking price as if there were no mortgage. When you buy the property, you're usually going to need financial help. You may go to a bank or a savings and loan or insurance company and buy it together with them. They put up part of the money and you put up part of the money. However, it is critical that you determine what the return is on the investment as an *all cash* deal before you commit yourself to borrowing money to buy the property.

Negative Leverage

To explain why, let's take a hypothetical case. Suppose that the return on the total investment without a mortgage is 6.5%. Suppose you have to borrow money to finance two-thirds of the purchase. Assume further that the best interest rate that you can get is 8%. The property is only paying 6.5%, so somebody has to make up that 1.5% extra needed to borrow the money. That somebody is you.

For example, assume you are putting up one-third of the purchase price and the bank is putting up two-thirds. You're getting 6.5% and the bank is getting 8%, resulting in a shortage of 1.5% that comes out of your share. But, it is worse than that! Since the bank is putting up twice as much money as you, you've got to come up with 1.5% on twice as much money as you have invested. Therefore, this is not a shortage of 1.5% against your share, it is a shortage of 3%. This means the return on your money is not 6.5%. It is 6.5% minus 3% or 3.5%!

Positive Leverage

However, leverage can also be positive and pleasant for you. Suppose the property is making 9% and you borrow the money at 8%. You're going to get 9% on your share and the bank is going to get 8% on its share. The extra 1% return on the bank's share goes to you. Since the bank's share is twice as big as yours, you are going to get 2% more. The happy result is that you're going to get 11% return on your portion of the investment. This is called positive leverage.

Positive leverage is why a lot of professional investors try to change the equity-mortgage ratio from one-third and two-thirds to 98% and 2% because it makes quite a difference. Of course, the one danger of doing it this way is that your equity is so small you have no staying power. If there is any trouble, the bank will foreclose on you quickly and you'll lose it all.

Capitalization Rule

After determining the annual net income, the next thing you are concerned with in the income approach equation (net annual income divided by the yield equals estimate of value) is the bottom part of the formula. That is, the yield rate, or return rate, or "capitalization rate." There are various ways of figuring this. Fundamentally, the objective is to find the rate that must be paid to attract money into this kind of an investment. There are a number of accepted ways of doing this. Let's review three of the most common ones.

Component Method

The first is called the "summation" or the "component method." It works this way. It sets forth four components that go into making up the capitalization rate and assigns a rate of return for each of these.

1. *Safe Rate.* The first of the components is what is called the "safe rate." This is the rate of return that you can get in the open market on a riskless investment. The rate that is usually selected is the rate of return on Series E Government Bonds.

2. *Nonliquidity Rate.* The next component is the "liquidity penalty" or "nonliquidity rate." Investments in real estate are not liquid. You can't call up a real estate broker with a sell order and then go down the next afternoon to pick up the check. It takes time to convert real estate into cash. What penalty do you charge real estate for being nonliquid? It will vary with the times, but currently it is about 2% in most parts of the country.

3. *Management Rate.* The fact that you have to manage property requires additional work and worry. If you had your investment in government bonds, you'd have no management. That means real estate deserves a bigger return.

4. *Risk Rate.* Finally, there is the "risk rate." This is a rate based on the chance that you will lose your entire investment. What's the risk you're taking? If you invested in government bonds, there is no chance you're going to lose your entire investment. If you're investing in real estate, there is the chance that you're going to lose your capital investment. That risk requires some financial consideration.

Add the percentages of these four components together and the total is the capitalization rate for this particular type of property.

To illustrate how this component or summation method works, here is the way you might compute it in a hypothetical case. The percentage rates used are for explanatory purposes only and would not be correct for every property and for every point in time.

Safe Rate	4.15%
Nonliquidity Rate	2.00%
Management Rate	1.00%
Risk Rate	1.50%
Total	8.65%

In this example, the indicated capitalization rate would be 8.65%. In other words, it would take a net return of 8.65% to attract investment money into this particular investment at this time.

Band of Investment Method

Another method commonly used is called the "band of investment method." This takes into account that not everyone who owns some kind of interest in real estate will be satisfied with the same rate of return on his investment. For example, the owner may regard his position as more risky than that of the second mortgage or first mortgage holders. He may, therefore, require a higher return than, say, the first mortgage holder would.

The idea of the band of investment method is to take each portion of a property's ownership or interest and multiply it by the rate of return required to attract money into that type of ownership position. By adding up all of the resulting products, you then get one overall capitalization rate that should apply to that particular property at that particular time.

For example, suppose the bank had a mortgage equivalent to half the value of the property. In addition, suppose Mr. Jones held a second mortgage equal to one-quarter of the value of the property. That would leave the owner—let's call him Mr. Green—with the remaining one-quarter of the property's value as his equity.

Let's assume that the bank wants 7% on its money, Mr. Jones wants 8%, and Mr. Green wants 10%. Then, you would have:

	Portion of Property's Total Value		Interest Rate Required		Product of Two Other Columns
The Bank (First)	.50	×	7	=	3.5
Mr. Jones (Second)	.25	×	8	=	2.0
Mr. Green (Equity)	.25	×	10	=	2.5
Totals	1.00				8.0

In other words, the overall capitalization rate in this instance would be 8%. Now, if you repeat this same process for a number of properties in a given area where you can gather accurate information about mortgage interest rates and the general return investors require on their equity, you can establish a pattern of capitalization rates that is fairly valid and reliable.

Comparison Method

The "comparison method" is simple. You go into the marketplace and check what kind of return various properties similar to the one in which you are interested are yielding. In other words, you find out what the "going rate" is for the property. This is just like the comparison approach that was discussed earlier as one of the three approaches to an estimate of value.

An easy way to get the "going rate" in the marketplace is to rearrange the income approach formula. The income approach formula is: *annual net income* divided by *capitalization rate* equals *estimate of value.*

In that formula, we know the annual net income and we know the capitalization rate. The unknown figure is the estimate of value. However, if you are trying to find out what the "going rate" of capitalization is, then that becomes the unknown figure. What you need to know in that case is the estimate of value, which we can assume is the market price for which a property sold. In addition, you need to know the annual net income. Divide the annual net income by the estimate of value and you will get the capitalization rate on that particular deal.

If you work this out for a number of properties in the neighborhood, you will soon see a pattern of what the going rate is.

Let's use an example: Suppose you check five sales in the neighborhood and you find the following results when you divide the annual net income of each property by the sales price:

Property #1	Annual Net = $ 8,000.	Sales Price = $ 90,000.
Property #2	Annual Net = $11,000.	Sales Price = $120,000.
Property #3	Annual Net = $15,000.	Sales Price = $165,000.
Property #4	Annual Net = $28,000.	Sales Price = $300,000.
Property #5	Annual Net = $31,000.	Sales Price = $300,000.

By dividing the annual net income by the sales price of each of these properties, you get this kind of read-out on the capitalization rate that seems current for property in this neighborhood.

Property #1	.089 or 8.9%
Property #2	.092 or 9.2%
Property #3	.091 or 9.1%
Property #4	.093 or 9.3%
Property #5	.103 or 10.3%

Right away, you can see that it takes a net return ranging from 8.9% to 10.3% to attract money to this kind of investment. There are some obvious weaknesses in this method, such as not knowing all the details of the sale and what is behind the sale price.

Such things as forced sales, money pressure for other purposes on the seller, tax pressures, salesmanship, interfamily transfers, and so on could all affect the sales price. In addition, the terms of the sale will affect the price. Lots of cash for down payment drives the price down. Little cash down payment means higher sales price. Beyond that, inflation and secret knowledge about factors affecting the values in the neighborhood could also distort the sales prices. All these possibilities must be considered in both the comparison approach to the estimate of value and the comparison method of figuring out what the "going rate" of capitalization is in the area.

However if you can gather the data on a number of properties, many of these things will probably offset each other and you will see the pattern.

POINTS TO KEEP IN MIND

- *The appraisal of real estate is only an estimate.*
- *The comparison approach to appraisal of real estate is:*
  comparable sales + or − adjustments = estimate of value.
- *The cost approach to appraisal of real estate is:*
  land + depreciated improvement = estimate of value.
- *The income approach to appraisal of real estate is:*
  annual net income ÷ capitalization rate = estimate of value.
- *Annual net income is adjusted gross income minus operating expenses, repair and maintenance expenses, and fixed expenses.*
- *Capitalization rate can be determined by the component method, the band of investment method, and the comparison method.*
- *Positive leverage works for you and negative leverage works against you.*

···· 5 ····

How to Bargain
for the Best Price

Everyone wants to get a bargain when they buy. One wag has defined a bargain as a deal where both sides are sure they cheated each other.

The best way to get a bargain is to use the bargaining pattern to your advantage. The normal bargaining pattern runs like this: The seller starts out by asking a price. The buyer offers another lower price. The seller comes down a bit on his price. The buyer comes up a bit on his offer. If everything works out, this process leads to a deal. That's a normal bargaining pattern. Now, let's analyze some of the parts of this process and see how they can help us get a bargain.

Rock Bottom vs. Top Dollar

Both buyer and seller usually have a price in mind in terms of their own expectations and evaluation of the property. The seller will have set for himself a "rock bottom" price. The buyer will have set for himself a "top dollar" price. When we have a deal, the rock bottom price is at least as low as the top dollar price of the buyer; otherwise, there will be no deal. Usually, the buyer and the seller will meet somewhere in the middle between the buyer's top dollar price and the seller's rock bottom price. The result of their negotiation will be a sale.

Bargaining

Extensive studies have been made of the patterns of bargaining. They reveal those things which most experienced bargainers already know. They show that the largest concessions are made by the buyer and the seller early in the game. The seller will drop his price more in the early stage of negotiating than he will later. The buyer will come up higher early in the game than he will later in the bargaining.

As bargaining progresses over a period of time, the buyer and seller remain at their respective positions longer and longer. The seller might stay at his expectation point for 24 hours if he's got a deal brewing, and then drop to a next lower price. He might stay at this one for several days, and then drop to a lower price. In each case, each drop is a little bit less than the previous drop, and, in each case, he is staying a little longer. Time can defeat a deal if the buyer and seller become exhausted and get firm on their prices. This is important to consider when you're negotiating. This is the typical negotiating pattern but there can be disturbing influences that will alter it.

Disturbing Influences

The normal pattern is rational behavior. People don't always act rationally. They like to think they do, but they don't. Here are some of the disturbing influences that can change this pattern:

1. *Emotion.*

    Emotion is a disturbing influence in everything we do. In a deal, emotions that are generated from something entirely removed from the bargaining transaction may affect the bargaining pattern. A great personal tragedy or disappointment may change the whole attitude of a buyer or a seller. A great elation, victory, success, or happiness may change an attitude. You might find a seller or a buyer who is very elated about having made a killing in another deal or some happy event in his life. This might make him unduly generous. Disappointment or tragedy, of course, can have a similar reaction—except that it is negative.

2. *Tax Pressure.*

One of the major considerations in real estate investments is taxes. This is because of the tax advantages that are possible. However, in order to take advantage of some of these opportunities certain deadlines must be met. You may find a man who is under tax pressure to sell, and must settle right now, or you may find some other person with tax pressure to buy.

Consider the situation of a man who has had his property taken by the state for an expressway. If he takes the money that he receives from the government from this condemnation and reinvests it into a like property within one year (after the end of the tax year in which the property was taken) he pays no tax. Suppose he has been looking for 11 months and 21 days, and he hasn't found the right property until he found yours. He needs to make a deal immediately. He's not going to be too fussy about it because it's more important to avoid paying those taxes to Internal Revenue. In fact, he may be willing to pay a little more than the usual price because of the taxes he will save.

3. *Business Pressure.*

The seller might be in a jam. He may be in a bad business situation. He may have to sell to raise cash, or he may have purchased a property, not knowing that the key to the property was another parcel. He has to have the second property or the first one is useless. This is another kind of business pressure. It can upset the normal bargaining pattern.

4. *Misinformation.*

If you don't have the right information, you can destroy the bargaining pattern. You may take the word of an unauthorized person that a shopping center is going to be built across the street from your prospective property. You find people are very willing to sell their property. You buy, and then find out that there will not be a new shopping center. You were misinformed and it disrupted the normal pattern of bargaining.

5. *Capacity.*

Some people are not mentally capable of making a deal. That doesn't mean they should be in a mental institution. It just means they know nothing about business. Typical of this are the people who own 60%

of America and control another 45% of it—women. There are a great many men who, after death, leave a lot of property to their widows. These women often are lacking in any kind of business experience or business knowledge. As a result, they will listen to all kinds of advice, often bad advice. The same problem exists with a number of people who are able to earn large sums of money but who can't manage it well. Medical men and entertainers are examples.

6. *Financing.*

Financing is very important because a deal is rarely made for all cash. If there is exceptionally fine financing, that can change the bargaining pattern. A man may say that he wants $50,000 for his property. The property next door may also be priced at $50,000. One seller will sell it to you for $1,000 down, and he'll take back a second trust deed for the $49,000 at 5% interest. The man next door wants $10,000 cash. He'll take the balance on the first trust deed, which means you can't build anything on it. He also wants it paid off in three years at 10%. He may not make a sale at $50,000. If so, it will probably only be after the first property has sold.

Price Limits

I said that the buyer has a rock bottom price that he expects to pay. The seller has a top dollar one that he won't go over. However, these things can be changed, too. The position of the rock bottom price or the top dollar price can be changed by some of the emotional factors we mentioned earlier.

Another thing that will change it drastically is the introduction of "straw men" into the negotiations. After experiencing several unsuccessful attempts to sell his property, the seller will often change his price limits. These disappointments cannot be with the same person, but with different people. Suppose the seller had $35,000 firmly in mind as his rock bottom price. Along comes prospective buyer number one, and the highest price he offers is $28,500. The seller refuses the offer. The next buyer offers $29,750 and is also refused by the seller. About this time, the seller is ready to shift his expectations—to a lower level. Then the next man offers $30,000. The seller may just accept the offer. The truth may be that the first two "buyers" were really working for the third man. This is called the introduction of "straw men."

Conversely, sometimes there are sellers, who in the course of negotiations, will whip out a signed, written offer to buy the property at a price that is higher than the seller anticipated. The prospective buyer's first question is why doesn't the seller take it. The seller may tell him he wants to have a 30-day escrow, and that the signed offer calls for a six-month escrow. He'll make other excuses as to why he doesn't want to accept the offer. The buyer then decides that he had better move if he is going to get the property, so he ends up eagerly offering more than originally planned. The buyer may never learn that the signed offer was a phoney or made by the seller's cousin.

Agents

It is an established fact that the best deals customarily are made when the buyer and the seller never see each other. If they do, it is after the deal is closed. There are a lot of reasons why this is generally true. Too many times there are personality clashes between the buyers and sellers. This would be classed as emotional, irrational behavior. It should be avoided. A good way to avoid it is to have a representative handle the negotiations. Communication between buyer and seller is much better because it is not interrupted by emotional factors. The broker can soothe irritations and find solutions to roadblocks because of his experience in negotiating. He is able to make suggestions that the seller and buyer might miss due to their personal involvement.

POINTS TO KEEP IN MIND

- *The biggest concessions are made at the beginning.*
- *Normally, both negotiators start with a rock bottom and a top dollar figure in mind. A deal is usually made at a point between these two extremes.*
- *Several things can disturb the normal bargaining pattern. Watch for them. Use them to your advantage if possible.*

    –Emotion.
    –Tax or business pressure.
    –Misinformation.
    –Lack of capacity.
    –Financing circumstances.

- *Straw men can distort price limits. Watch out for them.*
- *Face-to-face negotiations rarely work well.*

III

FINANCING
REAL ESTATE INVESTMENTS

••••6••••

Borrowing Money
on Real Estate

When you buy a piece of real estate, you're almost always going to need a loan to finance the purchase. There are two kinds of loans. There is the "interim loan" and the "take-out loan." These have other names, too. The interim loan is sometimes called a "construction loan." This is because it is used in connection with construction. The take-out loan is sometimes known as the "permanent loan."

The Interim Loan

Many lenders, like savings and loans or insurance companies, are prohibited by law from lending on a property that doesn't exist. That seems reasonable doesn't it? You may want to build a 60-

story office building on the corner. The long-term lender, often an insurance company, says he will give you a letter of commitment. You then go to a bank and say that you have an insurance company that will lend money on the building if you can build it and make it exist. The bank will ask to see the loan commitment in writing. You show them that the insurance company will lend this amount of money. The bank will then lend you the money on a temporary or an interim basis. That is why it is called an interim loan. When the building is completed, a permanent loan is made and is used to pay off the bank's temporary loan. This takes the bank out of the deal. This is where we get the term "take-out" loan.

Profit and Tax Considerations of Loans

There are some tax considerations in loans which we should touch on briefly. In terms of borrowing money on real estate, most professionals want to borrow as much money as possible. Take this example: You ask a landowner if he will sell you the property for $10,000 and subordinate a balance of $90,000. That means the landowner will take the balance of his deal back in a second trust deed or second mortgage. You have put $10,000 in it so far.

Then, you go to the insurance company and get a $300,000 loan commitment. You then go to the bank and get a construction or interim loan. You build the six-story building—you now have a $400,000 project going. Your total involvement is $10,000. Frequently, you can make enough on the deal before the building is finished so if it gets into difficulties, you can simply walk away from it.

A builder-developer will make a lot more than $10,000 out of the construction job. He normally should get 10 to 15% of the construction cost for overhead and office expense. That 10 or 15% is written into the price of the construction—plus 10% profit. Thus, the builder-developer might have 20 or 25% leeway over the actual cost of the building. So if it gets a little tight, he can walk away from it.

Assessment Dates

Many times builders will schedule their building to be finished after the day of the year that tax assessments are made. They'll schedule it so as much as possible it will be finished after that date. That gives them a tax break until the next year because the building taxes will not be at full assessed value for another year.

Trust Deeds or Mortgages

When you sell property, the papers can't say "second trust deed" or "first trust deed," they just say "trust deed." Whether it is a first or a second normally depends on the date it is recorded. The first one recorded has the first claim against the property, and the second one recorded has the second claim. However, when a piece of property is sold to a builder who is going to borrow money to build, the bank's trust deed has to be recorded first. By law the bank can't lend on anything except with a first trust deed. This is true even though the bank's trust deed will be recorded after the seller's. So the seller must agree in writing that his trust deed is subordinate or junior to the first trust deed of the bank. And, of course, the same thing is true if a mortgage is used instead of a trust deed.

Notes, Mortgages, and Trust Deeds

When you borrow money, you sign a note which evidences your debt. When you borrow money on a secured basis, you sign a note for the money. Then to secure that note, you will put up a piece of real estate as collateral. A mortgage or a trust deed is evidence that the property is collateral for the note.

Mortgage = Two Parties

Normally, a mortgage is an agreement between the borrower and the lender that the property will be the security. If the borrower defaults on a mortgage, the mortgage holder will declare a default. The borrower then has one year in which to bring the payments up to date. The mortgage holder cannot foreclose for that year. If he forecloses and then sells the property, he cannot give the buyer a deed signed by the recorded owner. He will give a "sheriff's deed." On a sheriff's deed there is at least another year period of redemption. This means that the original borrower can come back any time a year after the foreclosure and pay up all the past payments, penalties, and interest, and take the property back. A new buyer might not want to buy when he knows that the original owner can come and take the property away from him any time within that year.

Advantage of Mortgage

The major advantage to a mortgage is that, if there is not enough money coming out of the sale of the property to pay off the mortgage holder, he can get a judgement against other property the owner may have. This is called a deficiency judgement.

Trust Deed = Three Parties

In a trust deed you have three parties. There is a lender, a borrower, and a third party called the trustee (not to be confused with the trust deed). The borrower gives a deed that is already signed to the trustee. This empowers the trustee to sell the property and deliver that deed to anybody who buys it at foreclosure. Under a trust deed, the borrower usually has three months to make up past due payments. Three months could be more or less than 90 days. At the end of the three months, the trustee advertises the property for sale for 21 days. On the twenty-first day he auctions it off. The person that buys it will get a deed signed by the old borrower (owner). Because the owner gave the trustee a signed deed at the time he borrowed the money, there is no problem. He cannot come back and redeem it. The strength of the trust deed is the security of the deed and the speed with which it can be foreclosed.

Disadvantages

The weakness is that if the property doesn't sell for enough to cover the note, one cannot get a deficiency judgement against any other assets of the borrower. However, most trust deeds give the lender the right to elect whether he wants to foreclose as a trust deed or as a mortgage. He may have watered the price or the market may have dropped. If the property was sold today, it wouldn't cover the amount of money loaned against it. Therefore, the lender may elect to go the long route and foreclose as a mortgage. If the original price was not watered and the market has held firm, the lender will probably foreclose the property under the short trust deed route.

The Lender's Three Tests

When lenders consider a loan application, they usually apply three tests that will rate their risk when they lend money. They will rate the borrower, the property, and the location.

And when I say "risk," I mean their chances of losing the money they're lending you. They rate the borrower. What is his record of paying his bills? They rate the property. Is the value in the property? And what about the location? The property may be beautiful, but it is in a run-down neighborhood. So they rate these three things in terms of the risk of their investment: How sound is the borrower, the property, and the location?

POINTS TO KEEP IN MIND

- *Some developers make money even if the project goes broke.*
- *The difference between the construction or interim loan and the permanent or take-out loan is one of time and terms.*
- *Two-party mortgages and three-party trust deeds both have advantages and disadvantages. The trust deed is faster and cleaner, but you cannot get a deficiency judgement in most states.*
- *Most lenders apply a three-way test of risk before making a loan through which they rate the borrower, the property, and the location.*

7

Junior Financing and Nonmortgage Financing

Junior Mortgages

A junior mortgage is one that has a subordinate claim on the security. This claim may be a second, third, or lesser claim on the real estate collateral behind the first mortgage or trust deed.

Many experts agree that the junior mortgage plays a very important role in most real estate transactions. Some studies indicate that three out of four real estate transactions involve the use of some form of junior mortgage.

The vast majority of funds (or equity values) used for junior mortgages come from private individuals—often sellers of real property. Savings and loans and commercial banks provide some funds for junior mortgages but often

71

under another guise. Credit unions, corporations, investment trusts, etc. also are a source.

Use of Junior Mortgages. The junior mortgage is usually used in one of three kinds of situations. Although there may be other uses, these three are the most common:

1. *Noncash Payments.* As a way of paying a debt (often in connection with the property or a transaction involving the property) without using cash at the moment. Commonly given to real estate brokers, building contractors, materials suppliers, attorneys, etc.

2. *Reduce Owner's Equity.* The owner may want to convert part of his equity into cash for some other purpose, or he may want to increase his leverage position. He may want to convert a *paper* increase in the equity (due to appreciation of the property) into *cash*, or in a soft market, he may want to realize some cash until he can sell the property.

3. *Gap-Closer on Sales.* Normally, there is a gap between the sales price and the first mortgage balance. A portion of this gap is usually closed by the down payment. Often, however, the down payment doesn't close it completely. The junior mortgage is often used to close the gap completely and make the sale possible.

Characteristics of Junior Mortgages. In many ways junior mortgages are identical to first mortgages, but in some ways they are significantly different. The most important of those differences are:

1. *Relationship with First Mortgage.* The holder of a junior mortgage usually is entitled to the remaining proceeds of a foreclosure only after the first mortgage and costs have been paid. He does have the right to assume payments on the first mortgage himself and to foreclose on the property itself.

2. *Rates and Risk.* The risk involved is higher than that involved in a first mortgage usually. Therefore, the rates are higher, both nominally and actually. On junior mortgages, the nominal rates generally range from 7 to 10%. When coupled with the usual discount at which they sell (ranging from 20–50%—sometimes more), the effective rate of interest is quite high.

3. *Periodic Payments.* Typically, the regular (usually monthly) payments on a junior mortgage do not amortize the loan. The end result is that a substantial payment (called "balloon payment") is required on the last payment date.

4. *Term.* Most junior mortgages are short term in nature. Three to five years is typical in California. More than five years is unusual and a fully amortized term ("till paid" basis) is relatively rare.

Nonmortgage Types of Real Estate Financing

There are a variety of ways to gain care, custody, and control of real estate without using mortgage financing. However, most of these ways are open only to large financiers, very strong tenants, or substantial institutions.

Equity. The first obvious alternative to mortgage financing is to put up all the money oneself—buy the entire equity for all cash.

1. *Individual Equity Financing.* One approach is for an individual to put up all the money by himself. This has some drawbacks, however:
   a. Difficult to raise substantial sums of money.
   b. Individual usually lacks protection against unlimited liability in connection with investment.
   c. Harder to sell out all of equity.
   d. One man takes all the risk by himself.
2. *Syndicate Equity Financing.* The term "syndicate" is a popular way of referring to some form of joint method of equity financing with a number of participants. Many people seem to think that a "syndicate" is some form of legal organization. This is not true. With variations, there are only two forms of multiple legal organizations: partnership and corporation. A "syndicate" is, therefore, some form of partnership or corporation. There are many variations on the theme, such as general partnerships, limited partnerships, corporations, subsection "s" corporations, a partnership of corporations, etc.

   The advantages and disadvantages of a syndicate are varied, depending on the precise form adopted. Generally, the syndicate has these advantages:

   a. Easier to raise money.
   b. Easier to transfer all or part of the equity.
   c. Frequently, has perpetual life (except if a general partnership).
   d. The participants have limited liability.

   On the other side of the coin, there are generally these disadvantages:

   a. Participants have limited control of project.
   b. Disputes can arise among the participants (or their wives) that threaten the cohesiveness of the project.
   c. Often, there is double taxation of profits.
   d. It is not as easy to transfer partial ownership as it appears, since few people want to buy into a minority position.
   e. In the event of the death of one of the participants or a major dispute, the entire project might get tied up in a lawsuit (maybe

legitimate or maybe a spite suit) that could draw on for years and destroy the possibility of a profit.

Commercial Loan. Another approach is to secure a straight bank loan and use the proceeds to purchase real property without using the real property as collateral. This involves borrowing against the credit of the borrower or the borrower putting up some other kind of security. He might, for example, put up stock, bonds, personal property, etc. This approach is generally rather limited and available only to borrowers of great substance.

Bonds or Debentures, or Stock. It is possible for large, well-rated corporations to sell general obligation bonds or debentures to the general public in order to raise money to purchase real estate without using a mortgage. The corporation might also issue additional shares of stock.

Alternatives to Financing Real Property

In most cases, the main objective of real estate transaction on the part of a "buyer" is to gain care, custody, and control of the property on an exclusive or almost exclusive basis.

Instead of owning the property, there are a variety of other ways of achieving this goal. To a large extent, these other ways *might* reduce the need for financing.

Long-Term Lease. This provides a good approach, provided the property is *useable* as it is (or almost so). If the lessee is only leasing the land and has to pay for construction, it will probably require a larger investment than buying the property with a normal mortgage on it.

1. *Advantages of Leasing to a Tenant.*
   a. If the property is useable as is, it requires small capital investment.
   b. 100% of rent is deductible as expense. If property was owned, it could only depreciate the improvements.
   c. The money freed for other uses can frequently be used by the tenant in his own business at a greater profit.
   d. Reduces *tenant's* total debt load, leaving credit free for other borrowing.

2. *Advantages to Landlord.*
   a. Tenant will, during course of lease, pay what would have been the total purchase price several times over and the landlord will still own the property.
   b. Improvements to the property by the tenant usually revert to the

landlord at the end of the lease. The landlord's property is improved at the tenant's expense.

c. Tenant usually pays for all repairs and maintenance and all or part of the taxes.

d. Landlord gets advantages of depreciation deduction from his income tax.

e. If the property has been owned for a long time, the landlord would have had to pay a large capital gain tax upon sale. By leasing, he avoids paying this tax entirely.

3. *Disadvantages to Tenant.*

a. Often can't deduct depreciation on improvements, even if he makes them himself.

b. Doesn't share in the appreciation of the property, even though a good share of the appreciation is due to the tenant's presence.

c. Rent payments may be higher than the cost of an amortized mortgage.

d. If tenant has to make major improvement on property, he will probably invest more cash than if he owned the property and could get a mortgage.

4. *Disadvantages to Landlord.*

a. Often can't get strong-rated tenants willing to lease.

b. Leases are only as good as the people that sign them.

c. A tenant who is a good-rated tenant at beginning of lease may go sour in a few years.

d. Tenant may improve property with special-purpose development and then go broke (or worse, go broke before completing construction). Landlord is left with unsaleable and unleaseable property. He must spend a vast amount of money to correct situation.

Sales Contract (Land Contract). This is a device where the buyer comes into possession of the property under a sales contract, and after putting little or nothing down. He continues to have use of the property as long as he makes regular payments on the sales contract. The title to the property remains with the seller. After the buyer has paid in whatever buyer and seller originally agreed on to be paid, title is passed to the buyer.

These sales contracts are usually not recorded and go for a limited period of time (three, five, seven, or ten years).

Exchange. The use of the trade or exchange of properties is, in a sense, an alternative to mortgage financing. However, it might be argued that it really isn't since most of the properties involved in exchanges are mortgaged. However, the exchange does sometimes make a transaction possible without the use of additional financing or cash.

Sale Leaseback. Begun in 1939 by Safeway Stores, this has become a very popular technique among strongly rated companies with excellent credit. Other names for this form of transaction are "purchase lease," "sale lease," "lease purchase," and "leaseback." All these terms mean the same thing.

1. *Normal Procedure in Sale Leaseback.*

    a. Company buys property it wants and improves it as needed.
    b. Company sells property to major investor (most of the time a life insurance company, pension fund, or trust).
    c. Company leases property back for long term.

2. *Advantages to Seller-Lessee.*

    a. Get property exactly suited to own needs.
    b. Doesn't tie up working capital in fixed asset.
    c. Since leases are not considered long-term liability, rent is 100% tax deductible and lease term is often longer than mortgage term would be (for example, 99 years vs. 25 years), balance sheet looks better and credit is enhanced.
    d. Often more capital can be raised than by borrowing.
    e. Frequently, writing off 100% lease payments is better than depreciation since land portion of property cannot be depreciated.
    f. By selling property after development at a profit, seller-lessee gets use of additional cash today. He repays this in the form of rent over a long, long period in constantly inflating dollars.
    g. Often only the land is sold and leased back. Rent on the land is a deductible expense while retaining improvements for fast depreciation deduction.
    h. For companies working under government contracts that call for cost plus a fixed fee, rent is an allowable expense item but mortgage interest is not. This is why many aircraft, electronic, and other defense plants are leased rather than owned.

3. *Advantages to Buyer-Lessor.*

    a. Gets long-term, carefree investment.
    b. Gets appreciation value of property.
    c. Usually gets a yield on investment that is higher than he would in case of a mortgage.
    d. Lease payments will pay off original investment and lessor will still have title to a valuable property.
    e. Investment will not be paid off prematurely (as mortgages often are through refinancing). Investor will not have to go out seeking another good investment to replace the one prematurely paid off.

f. Deal usually requires a large amount of money. It costs the investor just as much (often less) to service one large investment as it does many small mortgages.

g. Lease terms often give lessor a claim against other assets of the lessee in the event of a default. This is better security protection than is available with a trust deed.

This whole area of leasebacks is so important that Chapter 9 will be devoted solely to that.

POINTS TO KEEP IN MIND

- *The junior mortgage is often used as a noncash payment for a debt, reducing owner's equity, and as a gap closer on sales.*
- *The junior mortgage is in a less favorable position than the mortgages ahead of it; is riskier and demands a higher rate of interest; is short term; and, usually requires a balloon payment.*
- *Ways to finance real estate without a mortgage include: equity money, commercial loans, and bonds, debentures, or stock.*
- *Other ways to control real estate without putting up too much equity money or borrowing mortgage money include long-term leases, sales contracts, and the sale leaseback.*

8

Tips About
Real Estate Syndicates

Forming a real estate syndicate is one popular way of financing, buying, and operating property. However, syndicates can be more than popular. They can be tricky. Too many people organize or get involved with a syndicate deal and come out sadder and poorer for the experience.

Over the years, I have been involved in a number of syndicates. When properly put together and managed, they work out well and everybody profits. When not properly put together and managed, they become a disaster!

In terms of organizing a syndicate, there are several things that you should keep in mind.

Syndicate Organization Factors

1. Age.

It is usually important that the members be all about the same age group. There are a variety of reasons for this, one of which is that different age groups have difficulty understanding each other and different generations have a background of varying experiences. For example, there are people who are mature enough to know what the Depression was all about. These people lost money and property. It made a lasting impression on them. If you mix people who remember the Depression with those who have no recollection of it, the two generations cannot communicate. This is especially true as far as investments are concerned.

2. Financial Status.

Their financial status should be comparable. It is not wise, in a syndicate, to get a mixture of very wealthy and very modest people. Everybody should be about the same financial status. The people don't have to be exactly the same net worth, but what you don't want is to put two men with a net worth of $500,000 each with a group of men that have a net worth of $20,000 each. If you do, there's going to be a tremendous lack of communication between these groups. What is peanuts to the man with $500,000, is a very substantial amount of money to the man with $20,000.

3. Objectives.

The aims of the syndicate and the individual members should be identical. There will be trouble if some syndicate members are interested in long-term appreciation and others only want tax shelters. Still others might feel it's vital that they have additional income right now. You will have trouble with these people because they have entirely different aims. Every decision concerning the property will present difficulties.

4. Personalities.

Only include people in the syndicate who obviously get along and whose personalities don't clash. It never works with all chiefs and no Indians. The objective of getting compatible personalities is very important.

5. Collect the Money.

Collect the money first. This is a cardinal rule. You have to get the money in hand before you start going out to invest it. Inevitably, if you don't, there's going to be one person who can't make it, not because he wants to let you down but because he has cold feet. The next thing is to find the investment. Do this only *after* you've got the money, because then you're more in a position to bargain. It takes too long to get the money together after the investment is located. There is then the chance that the investment is gone. I must emphasize that it is important for you to get the money first. Some will object to taking money out of their savings accounts, thus losing interest. It would be more convenient to take the money out of the savings account and put it into the syndicate's savings account and let it earn interest. This way it isn't in any individual's control. Get the money under the control of the syndicate before any investing is begun.

6. *Borrowing Money.*

Some investors will suggest that instead of putting up their money, the syndicate should get a bank to agree to loan the group money when an investment comes along. This may be possible, but it's very risky. Bankers change their minds from time to time. If it happens when you want that money, you may miss a good investment. A variation is to raise the money and put it into a savings account. Then, you find the investment. And, then, you borrow against the amount on deposit in your account in order to buy the investment. Some syndicate managers think this is good because the cash gives you some flexibility you wouldn't have if it was all tied up in the investment.

7. *Comparable Investment Shares.*

It is all right if all contributions are not *equal* amounts. However, it's unwise if the amounts are not *comparable*. You might get a situation where three people will put up $3,000, two others will put up $4,000, and one will put up $2,500. This is all right. What is not all right is where one or two men are putting up 50 or 75% of the money. When it comes to the time of a controversy, they will feel they have more authority since they have a bigger amount invested.

Syndicate Organization

Some people seem to think a syndicate is some special form of business organization—it isn't. It can be a partnership or a corporation; or, a combination of the two. In other words, a syndicate is just a gathering of people for a specific purpose. Namely, to invest in real estate. "Syndicate" isn't a legal term—it's a descriptive promotional term. When you form a "syndicate," you are actually forming a limited partnership, a corporation, or a combination. A combination would be when you have a partnership with a corporation.

As for the kind of legal organization that is best suited for your particular syndicate, that is something that depends on your best judgement and the advice of a competent attorney.

From a strictly business point of view, you might think about the pros and cons of each type of business organization as I have set them out below.

General Partnership

1. Everybody has an equal status in management.

2. Everybody is equally liable for the debts of the partnership. If everybody but you goes bankrupt, you are stuck with all the debts. Furthermore, in some states, if one of the partners goes bankrupt, those in the general partnership are secondarily liable for his *personal* debts. Better check the situation in your state with your attorney.

3. It's fairly hard to sell out your share if you want to get out of the arrangement.

4. If any partner leaves, dies, or drops out in any way, the partnership is dissolved and a new one has to be organized. Therefore, you would have to say that this form of doing business can be unstable.

5. It is relatively easy and inexpensive to organize.

6. There are income tax advantages. Partners can share in depreciation and profits can be distributed directly without the double taxation that you have in a corporate situation.

Limited Partnership

This is a variation on the theme of the partnership concept. In this arrangement, there need be only one "general partner." He is the one with all the powers and obligations of the partner described in the General Partnership section covered previously. All the other partners may be "limited partners." This means that their financial liability is limited to the extent of their investment only.

The problem with this arrangement is that none of the limited partners can have any say in the management of the syndicate property and the operation of the syndicate. If they do, they lose their status as limited partners and the protection of the limitation on their liability. Some limited partners don't like that.

Another problem of this arrangement is that somebody does have to take the rap and be the general partner. Someone must assume responsibility and liability for what goes on in the name of the partnership. One common solution to this problem is for the general partner to be a corporation. This provides a general partner, but one that has limited liability.

Corporation

The sole proprietor and the partnership are made up of "natural" people. The corporation is a "legal" person created by the state. As such, it has a life that is entirely separate and apart from any of its owners or managers.

1. It is easy to separate owners (stockholders) from those who operate the business (managers) even if they are the same natural persons.

2. The investors-owners (stockholders) have a liability for the debts of the corporation only to the extent of their investment.

3. It is often much easier to dispose of your share in the enterprise in a corporation than it is in a partnership.

4. The corporation, as a separate, state-created person, has a life that goes beyond that of the natural life of any of its owners. Therefore, it doesn't have to be reorganized every time some stockholder dies.

5. It is more complicated and more expensive to organize than a partnership, but that may be offset by the other advantages it has to offer.

6. It is not as advantageous from a tax viewpoint because—with one exception—depreciation cannot be passed on to its owners. Furthermore, as a separate person, the corporation must pay income tax on its income before it can distribute its profits. This cuts profits to the owners of the enterprise.

Subchapter s Corporations

As we noted, one of the major attractions of the corporate form of business organization is the limited liability. Few investors like to put their entire fortunes on the line for any investment. On the other hand, the corporate form in its normal structure burdens the investor with double taxation. In other words, the profits of an investment are first taxed while in the hands of the corporation, and they are taxed again when the corporation passes them into the hands of the individual investors who are corporate stockholders.

A possible way of getting the best of both these situations—that is, the limited liability of the corporation plus the avoidance of double taxation inherent in the partnership—is the "subchapter s corporation."

The subchapter s corporation is so named—clearly enough—because it is permitted under subchapter s of chapter 1 or subtitle A of the Internal Revenue Code. Officially, it is called a "small business corporation."

This is essentially a corporation (limited liability) that may elect not to be taxed as a corporation but—in essence—to be taxed like a partnership (no double taxation).

The organization of such an arrangement for any particular investor's needs clearly requires consultation with a tax attorney or an accountant and an attorney. It is not my function here to render advice on the suitability of a subchapter s corporation for any specific situation. However, it will be helpful, I believe, to mention some of the angles from a business viewpoint that you may want to consider.

Requirements

1. A new stockholder comes into the corporation who doesn't agree to not having the corporation taxed.
2. All the stockholders decide that it should be taxed as a corporation—in other words, if all the shareholders decide to drop their option.
3. The corporation no longer meets the qualifications of a small business corporation as spelled out under the "requirements" above.
4. The corporation gets more than 80% of its income from foreign sources.
5. After the first two years of operating, the corporation makes more than 20% of its income from such passive investment sources as rents, royalties, dividends, interest, annuities, or the sales and exchange of stocks and securities. Even in the first two years, such passive income cannot exceed $3,000 per year.

POINTS TO KEEP IN MIND

- *Syndicate member should be in the same age and financial bracket with identical investment objectives and compatible personalities.*
- *Always collect the money first and make the investment next. A syndicate operating on borrowed money is all right if done with care. Nobody should be significantly more invested in the syndicate than anyone else. Keep contributions comparable.*
- *Carefully consider which of the forms of organization best suit the members of your own syndicate:*
  –General Partnership—easiest to form, least permanent, unlimited liability.
  –Limited Partnership—limited liability to all but general partner.
  –Corporation—hardest to form, most permanent, limited liability.
  –Subchapter s Corporation—limited liability, no double taxation.

••••9••••

Leasebacks—What They Are and How They Work

There are many words in the English language that have more than one meaning. In fact, there are some words that have contradictory meanings —for example, the word, "dust." To dust something means to put a powder on— such as dusting one's back or dusting the roses. The word also means to take a powder off—such as dusting the furniture. And, of course, we also have more than one word or phrase that means the same thing.

An example of this is found in real estate investment. We have the "purchase leaseback" and the "sale lease-back." These are really both the same kind of transaction, but they are looked at from different points of view. In one case, the leaseback is seen from the point of view of a buyer, and in the other case, from the point of view of a seller.

Basically, what is involved is that an owner of a property sells the property and then leases it back. From his point of view, then, this is a "sale leaseback." From the point of view of a buyer, he is buying a property from the seller and immediately leasing it back to the seller. Now this may seem to be a somewhat strange transaction but actually it is not. It is a very sound type of real estate transaction and, in a way, it falls in the category of financing real estate. This is because it is a form of financial manipulation that is beneficial from a financial point of view and also from a tax point of view, to the parties involved.

Investors vs. Users

The rise of this kind of transaction in real estate began after World War II, although the first such transaction was probably in 1939. Since the second World War, we have seen a situation in the real estate market where you have a great many people who have control of vast sums of money for investment and are interested in investing in real estate, but only as an investment. By the same token, you have a great number of people who are interested in having the care, custody, and control of a piece of real estate but who are not necessarily interested in owning it. These are the users of the real estate, if you will, as opposed to the people who want to invest in it. So, you have a differentiation, or a dichotomy, between a user of real estate and an investor in real estate.

The investor in real estate is looking primarily for the highest possible return on his money with the great safety and longevity of investment, and the user is interested in having the use of the real estate with as low a financial investment as possible. Bringing these two objectives together, you have the sale leaseback and the purchase leaseback.

Background

The concept of the sale leaseback and purchase leaseback has a longer history in Europe than it does in the United States. It was probably common in European countries during the early part of this century. The first American transactions were started in 1939 between the Safeway market chain and private investors. Then, in 1942, the State of Virginia passed a law which allowed insurance companies, chartered in that state, to invest up to 5% of their assets in this kind of transaction. That led to the Life Insurance Company of Virginia buying a Washington warehouse from Safeway Stores and then immediately leasing it back to Safeway Stores.

During the next few years, most of the states passed similar laws which allowed insurance companies to make these kinds of purchase-leaseback transactions. The most important of the states, of course, to pass it was New York which is the home state of many large life insurance companies. The law was passed in 1946 by the New York Legislature, allowing their insurance companies to invest up to 5% of their assets in these kinds of transactions. Today, almost every state in the union permits it, although there are one or two that have it only on a restricted basis.

In addition to insurance companies that make this kind of lease transaction, there are now pension funds which are growing more and more important on the American scene as a source of investment money, as well as syndicates and individuals.

To counter the restrictions of the amount of assets that certain companies, such as insurance companies, may invest in leaseback deals, there is also a limitation by many states on the types of property that may be involved. For example, there are some states that forbid the use of the leaseback in the case of farming property, recreational property, or mineral exploitation property (such as oil wells, mining, etc.).

General Factors

There are several general factors that must be understood concerning leaseback transactions. There are specifics that vary from deal to deal but, generally speaking, the factors that we must look at include the strength of the seller-lessee, the terms of the lease, such things as renewal options and repurchase options, and the rent pattern.

1. *The Developer-Seller-Tenant.*

   A typical procedure would be for the user of the property to improve the property to his own specifications. He hires the contractor, constructs the building, and supervises it to see that everything is done to his satisfaction so that he's got just exactly the kind of property that he wants. This is particularly important for a user that is going to have some kind of special-purpose improvement put on the property. Maybe it's an extremely expensive laboratory or research facility, or some kind of specialized manufacturing facility that nobody else would ever want to use but that he uses exclusively. Then, having gotten the property exactly the way he wants it, he turns around and sells the property to an investor such as those mentioned previously. At the same time that he sells the property to the investor, he executes a lease with that investor to lease the property back.

2. *The Investor-Buyer-Landlord.*

Now, obviously, the investor, who is presently the landlord, wants to get a net rental that is high enough to give him a fair return on his investment and to pay off the cost of the improvement. Let's just say, offhand, that a situation exists where the land is worth $100,000 and the improvement is worth $200,000, so that the investor has to buy it for $300,000. Now, he wants a fair return on his investment of $300,000, whatever that may be, depending on the fair return in the marketplace at that time. Obviously, in a market where he can put his $300,000 into government bonds, treasury bills, or a savings account and accumulate 5 or 6%, he wants to earn more than that. In addition, he wants to pay off the cost of the improvement because it is depreciating with each passing day, is worth less and less, and will finally be worth zero at some point in the future. So, he wants to get back his capital investment.

Let's say an investor wants 10% return on his $300,000 per year, plus a write-off on the improvement. Let's also say that the improvement on the property is worth $200,000 and has a useful life of 20 years. Just using a straight-line depreciation concept, this means that he must get back $10,000 each year. So, that means he must get $30,000 a year return on his investment plus $10,000 recapture of the capital investment. Thus, in total, he must get $40,000 a year after all expenses are paid—$40,000 net, net, net.

3. *Tenant's Financial Strength.*

Because he is looking to the tenant to pay this $40,000 a year, the landlord wants to be sure that the tenant is capable of paying this. So, the financial strength of the tenant is an extremely important factor. A lease, as explained before, is only as good as the people who sign it. If the financial strength of this particular tenant is not good enough to guarantee that he is going to pay off $40,000 a year, after all other expenses, for the next 20 years, then this is not going to be a suitable transaction for most investors interested in leaseback deals.

4. *Renewal Options.*

Suppose at the beginning of the sale transaction, the tenant says,

Well, I'll sell the property to you, then I'll lease it back from you for 20 years. At the end of 20 years, you will have gotten back not only the cost of the building but also the return on your money. However, I'd like the option to renew and continue on with the property because it would still be useful for a few years beyond that, but I want it at a much lower rate of rent. In other words, you've gotten back your original investment in the building and I would like to renew at a lower rental rate. Say, instead of $40,000 a year net, net, net—$30,000, or $25,000, or something of that sort.

Well, that's a point of negotiation that has to be considered in various lights, depending on what the tenant's and the landlord's objec-

LEASEBACKS—WHAT THEY ARE AND HOW THEY WORK

tives are. It may turn out that the property is obsolete and, generally speaking, from the point of view of the investor, options are a one-way street. They tie the investor and they don't tie the tenant. In other words, the tenant may or may not renew, if he wants to—it's entirely up to him. If it's advantageous to him to renew, he may do so—if it's not advantageous, then he won't. So, obviously, the tenant is only going to exercise the option if it is good for him. From the point of view of the landlord, he's not interested in what's advantageous to the tenant, as such. He's interested in what's good for himself.

5. *Repurchase Option.*

One of the options that is sometimes sought in these kinds of deals is the right to repurchase the property. Generally speaking, this is prohibited by law in many states, and it's also prohibited by good business practice for the simple reason that people (like the Internal Revenue Service) say that this is really not a leaseback deal. This is simply a subterfuge to avoid paying taxes. That, actually, if A constructs the building and sells it to B and then A leases it back from B and has the right to buy it back from B at some predetermined price, then this is merely financial trickery designed to mislead everybody about what is going on. In fact, A is the owner, always has been the owner, and always will be the owner. So A is the one who we are going to hold responsible for the property. Now, there have been some modifications of this, whereby A had the option of purchasing the property but not at a fixed figure. In other words, if A just had the right of first refusal to match any other offer, that may be permissible. All in all, the option to purchase the property is a shaky thing and should not even be considered without careful consultation with an appropriate attorney.

6. *Rent Payment Pattern.*

Now, there is also the question as to what is the pattern of the rent? Generally speaking, we have two kinds of patterns. There is the so-called "high-low rent pattern" vs. the "level rent pattern." The high-low pattern is a sliding scale where payments start high and then, as you pay the rent off, it gets lower and lower. For example, there might be a situation where you get a 25-year lease and the seller-tenant says, "I will pay you 9% of the total investment cost the first 15 years of the lease and then 5% the last ten years." Actually, this is something that depends on the attitude of the landlord and the problems that the tenant might have.

The tenant might be starting a new line of business, a new product —the whole thing might be an experimental venture or it may be a kind of activity that is very expensive for him to get started in. Therefore, he wants to cut his operating expenses in the early part of the lease to a minimum by keeping his rent down.

So, that's all a matter of negotiation and whatever makes sense in developing a solid deal—one where you've got a good tenant you can count on to stay in business for the full term of the lease. Otherwise, you could very well end up with a special-purpose property that nobody else wants and that you have to write off as a loss.

Advantages to Seller-Tenant

Of course, all of this conversation really doesn't explain, "Why?" Why is it that users of real estate and investors in real estate want to engage in this kind of complicated deal? Obviously, the reason is that there are advantages to each side. What are these advantages? Let's first look at the advantages to the seller-tenant.

1. *Government Contracts.*

There are many companies involved in the space program or military programs who operate under government contracts. Under the terms of most of these government contracts, they get the cost of their production plus a fixed fee. The term "cost" is a little misleading because the government doesn't just give them a blank check and say, "We'll pay for whatever costs that you have." Rather, it agrees to pay for certain kinds of costs. If you incur costs other than these, that's your problem as a contractor. And, this is where the advantage of the leaseback situation has some weight for a government contractor, because rent is included in what normally is allowed as cost but interest is not. Therefore, if you were to borrow the money to build a plant, to fulfill your government contract, the interest on that mortgage is not deductible as an expense and it comes out of your profit. Whereas, if you rent the facility, by building it and then selling it and leasing it back, the rent is all deductible.

2. *Unfreezing Capital.*

The leaseback deal unfreezes the tenant's capital that he has tied up in the property. Even if he borrows money to erect the building that he is going to occupy, usually he still has a considerable amount of capital tied up in the property. By selling the property and leasing it back, he unfreezes this capital which gives him more working capital. Most companies are able to make a greater return on their working capital than they can on the property that they may occupy. For example, because of the nature of the property, a user of real estate frequently can't make more than 5, 6, or 7% return on the cash he's got invested in property that he, himself, occupies and uses. Whereas, if he controlled the cash that was tied up in that property and had it in the form of working capital, he might easily make 10 to 20% return on that cash.

3. *Improves Balance Sheet.*

When you are in business, having a good-looking balance sheet is important because you frequently have to go into the banks to borrow money for short periods of time to obtain working capital or for other important projects. By selling your real estate and by taking all your equity in that back in cash, your balance sheet has had two things happen to it that make it look very good.

Number one, it has reduced a fixed asset plus probably a long-term debt in the form of a mortgage, so that you can take a fixed asset and subtract that from your balance sheet, and you can subtract a long-term liability.

The second thing is that you have increased your cash. Now the reason that this is important is that bankers look at cash as being far more important than a fixed asset, because fixed assets are hard to evaluate and by their nature they are hard to liquidate to meet the demands of a loan if it should become due. So bankers look at what they call liquid assets, as opposed to fixed assets, and they like them much better. Bankers are willing to lend you money if you can prove to them that you have absolutely no use for it or need for it.

4. *New Plant.*

Another advantage is that this gives the seller-tenant a chance to get a new plant—one that is modern and up to date—and to do so without laying out any capital. The advantages here are obviously the same as those mentioned above in terms of keeping his balance sheet looking good and his working capital unfrozen. But, beyond that, it also gives him a modern facility which would enable him to operate— hopefully—more efficiently, make a bigger profit than he would have with his old plant, and do this without making a major capital investment.

5. *Profit on Leaseback.*

Another aspect is that it's not unusual for the seller-tenant to actually make a profit on the deal. In other words, he may buy the land for $100,000 and build a property on it for $200,000, so that his total investment is $300,000. Then, he might turn around and sell the whole package for $400,000 so that he makes $100,000 profit on the deal. Admittedly, he has to pay part of this profit in higher rent payments so that the investor will get an interest rate that is attractive to him, but the seller-tenant is getting $100,000 profit now in a lump sum and then paying that off to the buyer-landlord. Over a 20- to 30-year period, the natural course of inflation is going to decrease the purchasing power of that money which is coming in dribs and drabs across those many years. So, really, the seller-tenant is getting a marked advantage from that angle.

6. *Depreciating Land.*

One of the disadvantages in owning a property is that you are not allowed to depreciate the land because the Internal Revenue Service holds the theory that land cannot be depreciated. (This, in my opinion, is not always true.) In other words, if you owned a $300,000 property and $100,000 of it was land and $200,000 was improvements, you could only write off the cost of the $200,000 as depreciation. You could not write off the $100,000 that is represented by the land value. When the seller-tenant sells the entire package for $300,000 or $400,000, he can deduct the entire amount of his lease payments and, therefore, is, in effect, getting a tax deduction by virtue of being able to write off the lease payments that he would not be able to get if he owned the property and tried to depreciate it—because he couldn't depreciate the land.

Obviously, the higher the ratio of land value is to improvement, the better this angle is in the deal. And, in effect, what the seller-tenant is doing by writing off the land value by virtue of leasing it back, is getting Uncle Sam to pay for part of the cost of what he paid for the land. He thereby gives himself a return that he wouldn't get ordinarily.

7. *General Policy.*

There are some companies that prefer to finance by selling their property and leasing it back for no other reason than they choose to avoid having debts. There are a variety of reasons behind this. It could be just a personal philosophy of the management of the company. It could be, as indicated before, to improve their borrowing position at the bank. It could be that it gives them more freedom of action and, in terms of their own investments, provides a chance to have cash available to make investments as opportunities arise, rather than having all cash and capital tied up in fixed assets that they can't liquidate in a hurry. There are a variety of reasons for it.

8. *The Split-Sale Leaseback.*

For the more sophisticated operators, there is a growing trend to split the various kinds of equities in a property, keeping some and selling others. For example, you may have a situation where the party may own a shopping center and wants to keep the shopping center building so that he can write off the building depreciation. As a device to "write off" the land, he sells just the land to an investor and leases it back. In this way, he gets to write off the cost of the land by rent payments which are fully deductible and the cost of the building by depreciation deductions—and, as Dr. Pangloss in Voltaire's *Candide*, "have the best of all possible worlds."

Advantages to the Buyer-Landlord

With all these advantages to the seller-tenant, what possible reason could an investor have for entering into such a transaction? It looks, from the above, as if all of the pluses are on the side of the seller-tenant. As it is in all good business deals, this is not true. There are advantages from both sides, which is why the deals come about. Let's explore what some of those might be.

1. *Getting Good Tenants.*

     One of the problems that most real estate investors have—both large and small—is getting a good tenant for a property that they own. It's one thing to have a lovely store or factory building sitting empty, and it's another thing to have one occupied by a financially secure tenant who will live up to the terms of his lease (thereby giving you the kind of return on your property that you expect or hope for). In the sale-lease transaction (which we will now turn around to look at from the point of view of the buyer, and call it a purchase-leaseback transaction), the buyer-landlord is able to pick his tenant before he picks his investment. In other words, he finds the kind of tenant he wants to have before he has to pick the property. On a speculative basis, it is often the other way around. You buy a piece of land or a building and then you look around and hope for the right kind of solid tenant. This is something you don't have to do with the purchase-leaseback deal— you have a tenant built into the deal.

2. *Big Investment Opportunity.*

     As curious as it may seem to many people, it is frequently hard for institutions such as insurance companies and pension funds to place large blocks of money into a single investment. The reason that it is advantageous to put large blocks of money into a single investment is that it costs less time, effort, and investigation to make one large investment than it does to make ten small ones. So, if you can put your money to work in a simpler big investment, that is preferable to running around getting into ten or a score of smaller investments.

3. *Carefree Investment.*

     By the peculiar nature of the purchase-leaseback transaction, where you buy the property from the real estate user and lease it back to him on a net, net, net basis, you have a virtually carefree investment. That is to say, the tenant is responsible for all of the expenses of operating the property—maintaining it, paying the taxes, complying with all laws for operations of the property, etc.—and you simply have to collect your rent. If you have a good tenant, this is relatively easy in most cases. So, it's an attractive investment from that point of view.

4. *Reversion Right.*

Another advantage is that, at the end of the lease term, the purchaser-landlord ends up with a property that has substantial improvements on it—usually—and, without costing him anything. By this, I mean that he buys a building which may have 30 or 40 years of life left in it; leases it back to the user on a 20- or 25-year term—during which the entire cost of the improvement is paid off; then ends up with the building all paid for and still useful for another five to ten to 15 years. Therefore, anything he gets for the rental of that building, over and above the return on his investment, is profit.

5. *Inflation Hedge.*

As real estate has traditionally been for years, the purchaser-landlord has a terrific hedge against inflation because during the term of his lease deal, he is guaranteed by the tenant that he will get paid back a fair return on his investment plus the total cost of the improvement. In addition, if the value of the property inflates over the years— and history has indicated that this is the pattern in our country—he will end up with property that is worth substantially more than when he purchased it and yet is all paid for.

For example, let's go back to our hypothetical case where the land is worth $100,000 and the building is worth $300,000. The purchaser-landlord enters into a 20-year lease on which he's getting 10% return on the $300,000 plus $10,000 a year to write off the cost of the building. So, he gets a total of $40,000 a year for 20 years. At the end of 20 years, he has the building free and clear and has gotten a 10% return on his investment which means that his investment has been paid back twice in the 20-year period. Once each ten years it's paid back entirely. He then owns the property, which is, through inflation, probably worth $600,000 or $700,000. Contrast this with what would have happened with his $300,000 if it had been left in a savings account earning 5 or 6% interest. He would be much worse off because his 5 or 6% interest barely covers the erosion of the purchasing power of his money through inflation.

6. *Higher Return.*

It is not unusual in a lease transaction for the return on the investment of the purchaser-landlord to be higher than it would be if the seller-tenant were borrowing the money to get a mortgage on the property. The buyer-landlord is putting up 100% of the cost of the property as opposed to a bank, which would lend possibly between 50 and 67% on the value of the property, if it were to make a loan. So, there is a higher risk, as I indicated. Another factor is that leaseback deals are rather complicated and take a lot of time. The terms have to be specially tailored for each particular seller-tenant and buyer-landlord. This takes a lot more time than just granting a loan. Another thing is that a lease-purchase deal is usually not as saleable as a mortgage. If you have a straight mortgage on somebody's property and you want to raise cash on that, you can turn around and sell it in the open market or to another investor, etc., but a leaseback deal is not as easy to sell unless you can find another buyer-landlord who has the same kind of situation and needs that you do. Because of its tailor-made nature, the market is more limited. There are many other reasons, but that is fundamentally the situation.

Conclusion

The leaseback deal offers some unusual opportunities for many investors. It has been taken advantage of mostly, in the last 25 years, by large investors such as pension funds and life insurance companies. However, it does offer many opportunities to the small and modest investor—if he knows how to go about it the right way.

One of the reasons a small or modest investor, who may have anywhere from $10,000 to $100,000 to invest, has not gotten into leaseback deals is because he really isn't experienced enough to know about them and understand what is involved in them. He does not know the advantages and disadvantages or how to find a deal and put it together. This is not nearly as hard as many people make it out to be and it's an area that more investors should look into.

Leasebacks on a Modest Scale

For example, you might review the stable merchants and manufacturers in your own town—people who have been there for a long time and have a good, solid financial base in the community; a good credit rating—those who have done a good business. The enterprising investor will go to these kinds of tenants. They may be local tenants which, perhaps, makes them not as secure as a major corporation (although that's not always true either) but they do have a good stake in the community, and they are going to be there for a long time. Their name on a lease is meaningful and they can be trusted to honor their obligations. They have a good credit rating and a good record.

The enterprising investor will go to these people and say, "Look, why don't you release all this capital you've got frozen." Then, weigh the advantages discussed in this chapter and say, "Let me buy your store from you. Let me buy your little plant from you and lease it back to you. You'd have the care, custody, and control of the property as you always have had and yet you have all these other advantages available to you. It's a good deal for me *and* you."

Of course, don't forget that the buyer-landlord is in a position to put a mortgage on the property to assist himself in its purchase, so we are not talking about an all-cash purchase necessarily. You may be assuming a mortgage that's already on the property, or putting a new mortgage on it, so that you are only coming up with a part of the cash—one-third or 25%—and you will be borrowing, not on your own credit, but on the credit of the seller-tenant. Therefore, even if your credit isn't as good as his, the lender is looking toward that lease and the credit of the tenant more than he is to you and the value of the property, itself.

So, there are many opportunities that are available here for the small and modest investor—it's just unfortunate that he doesn't take advantage of them.

POINTS TO KEEP IN MIND

The sale leaseback or purchase leaseback (same thing from a different viewpoint) offer many opportunities to both investors and property users.

- *Generally, for the deal to make sense, the requirements of the developer-seller-tenant and the investor-buyer-landlord must be considered. Some of the factors to weigh include tenant's financial strength; renewal and repurchase options; and, the rent payment pattern.*
- *Advantages to the seller-tenant include:*
  –Government-contract tenants get a better deal.
  –Capital is freed for more profitable uses.
  –Balance sheet looks better.
  –Get modern plant.
  –Enables making a profit on the sale leaseback.
  –It's a way to "depreciate" land.
  –It permits split-sale leasebacks.
- *Advantages to the buyer-landlord are:*
  –A way of getting a superior tenant.
  –Provides opportunity for large investment.

--*Often is a relatively carefree investment.*
--*Reversion right gives the landlord an improved property at the end of the lease.*
--*Hedge against inflation.*
--*Higher return on invested capital possible.*

IV

ANALYSIS OF
REAL ESTATE INVESTMENTS

···10···

Financial Analysis—
Key to Intelligent Investing

Financial reports play an important role in real estate financing. They give the lender a quick summary of the financial condition of the borrower and his prospects. For the single-family residence borrower, there are just two or three reports that are of prime concern. For the borrower involved in some form of income or investment property, there are a number of additional reports that should be considered.

Two Weaknesses

There are at least two major weaknesses in the use of reports as a basis for financial decisions by the lender that we must recognize:

101

1. *Past, Present, and Future.* Many financial reports, including the two most common, are statements of the financial activities and condition of the borrower *in the past or at the present moment.* The lender's primary concern is *the financial future of the borrower.*

It is possible, for example, for a prospective borrower to have had a marvelous financial past up to this moment and for him to then go bankrupt 30 days after the new loan is granted him. Reports of the past do not tell the lender that the borrower is going out of business next year because of a technological change; or, about his personal life which could change his entire set of prospects; or, about the myriad of other factors that may completely change the borrower's financial status and which are completely unpredictable.

Some reports attempt to see into the future. However, looking into the future more than a year or two becomes a very hazardous thing. This, in spite of the fact that the lender is committing the use of his money for a period of many years in the future. As some wag once said, "He who lives by a crystal ball is doomed to eat broken glass."

2. *Lender's Astigmatism.* Another major weakness in the use of financial reports is that an alarming number of loan officers in financial institutions do not really understand how to read them. As a result, there is an almost slavish dependence on "rules-of-thumb" and rigid formulas.

For example, the lender may have a rule-of-thumb for the current ratio (explained in detail in a moment) of 2 to 1. Looking at the balance sheet of prospective borrower "A," the lender sees a current ratio of 2.1 to 1. Looking at the balance sheet of prospective borrower "B," the lender sees a current ratio of 1.99999999 to 1. Does he accept borrower "A" and reject borrower "B"? Suppose it later develops that borrower "A" is a secret alcoholic which resulted in his losing his job a year later? The financial report doesn't reveal (or even whisper) this fact at the time the loan is considered, but, looking back, who would have been the better borrower, "A" or "B"?

The purpose of this example is not to be cute or clever, but simply to point out the problem of absolute reliance on ratios, formulas, and financial reports, when dealing with something so complicated and unpredictable as people.

ACCOUNTING PRIMER

As indicated, there are several types of reports in common use and these will be reviewed briefly here. However, it is necessary to first understand a few basic facts about the most popular accounting system in use today. It is the "Double Entry System." As the name implies, it is based on the concept of *making two entries in the books to record each transaction.* The "books" actually consist of a series of "accounts." Each account represents one portion of the total financial structure of the borrower. For example, the money he has in cash is recorded in the account labelled, "Cash;" the money that other people owe him is recorded in the account labelled, "Accounts Receivable;" the money that he owes other people is recorded in the account labelled, "Accounts Payable;" and so on for everything he owns, he has due him, or he owes other people. The sum total of all these various accounts equals the books.

Each account has two sides; a left side and a right side. By common agreement, some accounts are increased by making an entry on their left side. These same accounts are decreased by making an entry on their right side. With other kinds of accounts, the reverse is true. They increase with right-side entries and decrease with left-side entries. Professional accountants have special names for the two sides of an account. They call the left side the "debit side" and the right side the "credit side." An entry on the left side of an account is a "debit" and an entry on the right side is a "credit."

As mentioned previously, the heart of the double-entry system is the business of making two entries for each transaction. *One of these entries must be a credit and the other must be a debit.* Most people have heard the term "balancing the books." This simply means that the total of all the debits in all the accounts equals the total of all the credits in all the accounts.

Further, accounts are divided into one of five categories:

1. *Assets Accounts.*
   Things the borrower owns.
2. *Liability Accounts.*
   Debts and claims against the assets of the borrower.
3. *Capital Accounts (also called "net worth").*
   The difference between the borrower's assets and his liabilities. In other words, that portion of his property that he owns free and clear of any debts or claims at the moment.
4. *Expenses.*
   What he spends during a specific period of time.
5. *Income.*
   What he receives during a specific period of time.

As mentioned before, there is a common agreement as to whether a debit entry in an account will increase or decrease the value of that account. The basis of the determination is which of the five categories does the account belong to?

A debit entry *increases* the value of all asset and all expense accounts.

A credit entry *increases* the value of liability, capital, and income accounts.

An easy way to remember is with the little chart of "ALICE."

CREDIT	*Account Category*	DEBIT
— minus	A (Assets)	plus +
+ plus	L (Liability)	minus —
+ plus	I (Income)	minus —
+ plus	C (Capital)	minus —
— minus	E (Expense)	plus +

Basic Types of Reports

By taking the accounts in the five categories into consideration, a basis for the two most widely used and fundamental financial reports can be formed:

1. *The Balance Sheet.*

   The balance sheet tells you the financial condition *as of one moment in time.* It tells you what is owned, owed, and what's left.

   Assets are one-half of the report. Liability and capital together comprise the other half of the report. Both halves must "balance" or equal each other. Assets equal liability plus capital.

   Assets is the sum of all that is owned. Liabilities shows the portion of assets belonging to your creditors. Capital shows the portion of assets belonging to you.

2. *Operating Statement.*

   Also, called the "Profit and Loss Statement," this is a summary of financial transactions *over a period of time.*

   Income is one-half of the report. Expense is the other half. These will *not* balance except in that rare case where one just "breaks even." Usually one will be greater than the other. If income is greater than expense (the universal goal), the difference is called "profit." If expense is greater than income, the difference is called "loss."

   There is a relationship between these two types of reports. The profit or loss from the "Operating Statement" is posted directly to the "Capital" and "Assets" sections of the balance sheet.

If there has been a profit, some assets (cash, receivables, investments, real property, etc.) will have increased to reflect this. At the same time, there will be a commensurate increase in capital.

Pro Forma Reports

When the loan under consideration is for a project to be built, the borrower obviously cannot present operating statements on which to judge past performance—there hasn't been any. In this instance, it is common to require that *estimates of future performance* be made. This is usually done by preparing "Pro Forma Financial Statements," which are reports predicting how operations will work out. Pro forma reports basically differ from operating statements and balance sheets, showing you past performances, in that the account titles are preceded by the word "estimated" (estimated income, estimated expenses, etc.).

Supplementary Reports

In addition to the two basic types of financial reports, there is a growing trend toward the use of additional reports that provide more information or a more detailed analysis. Some of these supplemental reports can be quite helpful in making a sound judgement on the character of a loan application. However, there is the ever-present danger that these additional reports may fall into the "fad" category and be called for by loan officers who do not really understand their full significance. This is bad enough in itself but the real danger lies in the smug feeling of overconfidence that such sophisticated reports may engender. The result could be that these supplementary reports might produce *fewer sound loans* rather than more sound loans.

In other words, they are valuable when prepared properly and accurately and when used by personnel who clearly understand them. Otherwise, they are not valuable, and may possibly be dangerous.

Some of the more important such supplementary reports include:

1. *Source and Use of Funds.*

   This report shows where the money came from and where it went on the balance sheet. For example, it is possible that two balance sheets a year apart will both show exactly the same ending totals. One might assume, therefore, that there has been essentially no significant change in the financial condition. This is not necessarily true. The *internal structure* of the balance sheet might have changed dramatically, yet still gives the same totals. This structural change might seriously affect liquidity, ability to repay loans, or willingness to repay loans. The searching loan officer wants to know about such internal structure changes. The "Source and Use of Funds Statement" helps him know.

As indicated, this SUF statement tells where the money came from and where it went. It has two sections: "Source of Funds" and "Use of Funds." The totals of both sections should be the same.
The rule to remember is this:

Increase in liability, or
decrease in asset $\left.\right\}$ is a SOURCE of funds

Increase in asset, or
decrease in liability $\left.\right\}$ is a USE of funds

When you think about this for a moment, it will become very obvious to you.

2. *Rent Schedule.*

In the case of income property, an important report is a certified "Rent Schedule" that sets forth what the monthly rentals are; the names of each tenant; the basis of his tenancy; when the rent is paid and to whom; the amount and type of advance payments (security deposits, cleanup deposits, etc.); and so on.

This schedule should be notarized and warranted as to its completeness and accuracy by the borrower. It has not been useful in the past but it is worthy of consideration, that the rent schedule also show any concessions that may have been made to the tenant such as free rent, television sets, moving expenses, etc. These factors may seriously affect the stability of the rental income. The wise loan officer or buyer also makes it a point to check very discreetly the details of their tenancy with the tenants. For example, it may be completely true that tenant "A" pays $175 per month for his apartment. It may also be that tenant "A" gets every twelfth month free as an inducement to remain there. There is nothing wrong with this in itself, unless the loan officer or buyer is led to believe that the annual income from that apartment is $2,100 ($175 × 12) when, in fact, it is actually only $1,925 ($175 × 11).

3. *Inventory.*

In the case of income property, there may be a substantial number of items of personal property. There should be an inventory of these. This might be obvious in the case of, say, a furnished apartment building. It would not be so obvious, however, in the case of an unfurnished apartment building. In this last instance, there still could be several thousands of dollars in personal property and equipment on the premises; such as, television sets, recreation room equipment, patio and pool furniture, commonuse vacuum cleaners, laundry room equipment, etc.

4. *Break-Even Chart.*

For some reason it is rarely used or thought of, but it can be an important tool in financial analysis. It is a graphic representation of the relationship among income, fixed costs, and variable costs.

The term "income" is self explanatory but the other two may require additional clarification. To operate an income property, it requires the expenditure of certain basic funds just to keep the doors open. This has nothing to do with the number of tenants nor how much space is rented. These expenses (real estate taxes, insurance, interest on mortgages, etc.) go on and on whether the property is 100% leased or 100% vacant. These are called "fixed expenses."

The other category, "variable expenses" will occur in direct proportion to the extent the property is leased. They are at their highest when the property is 100% leased and at their lowest when the property is 100% vacant.

Figure 10-1, which follows, shows how a break-even chart would work using a 50-unit apartment house as an example.

FACTS: 50-unit apartment house . . . going rental rate in marketplace

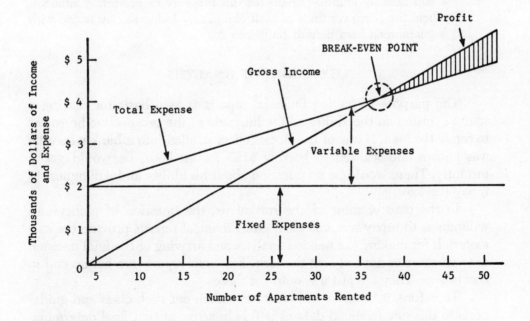

Figure 10-1. *Monthly Break-Even Chart (50-Unit Apartment House).*

= \$100/month. Fixed expenses (taxes, loan interest, insurance, etc.) = \$2,000. The variable cost of operating each apartment when rented is \$50/month over and above the fixed expense.

It only takes a glance at this break-even chart to see immediately that 37 apartments must be rented to break even. The first profit comes with the rental of the 38th apartment.

An important point that this kind of analysis makes, very dramatically lays to rest one of the oldest and most unfortunate myths about income property. This falsehood is: If the building were 100% rented, it would yield 10% of the monthly income as profit. The foolish and unwary automatically assume that this means there is \$10 profit in \$100 rent of the *first* apartment. This is not true! The profit comes at the end of the rent schedule and not before. The building used in this example doesn't show 1 cent profit until 37 apartments (or 74% of the total building) is rented.

The loan officer or investor, in reviewing such a chart, must answer this important question: Are the product (the apartments) and the market conditions such that the building will be 74% sold (rented) at all times?

If the answer is, "no," the loan officer or investor may be buying himself a bad deal by granting credit for this property or project. A situation where the borrower finds himself chronically losing money is one with a guaranteed loan default built into it.

THE TOOLS OF ANALYSIS

The purpose of having financial reports is as a basis for making a sound decision on the ability and willingness of the prospective borrower to repay the loan. If one of the Rockefellers strolled into a bank where he was known and wanted to borrow \$125 for an hour, he would get it instantly. There would be no question about his ability and willingness to repay the loan.

In the case of most of the rest of us, the question of ability and willingness to repay is not so clear cut. Financial reports provide the *raw materials* for making the needed analysis and arriving at the final decision as to whether or not to grant the loan. *Financial reports are not an end in themselves.* They are just a way to get there.

Therefore, it becomes important to search out such clues and guideposts in this raw financial data as will help arrive at that final determination.

The tools of analysis that are most commonly used fall into four categories: liquidity, leverage, activity, and profitability. The *ratio* is the common measuring stick; that is, how much of "A" to how much of "B"?

Liquidity

Study of "liquidity" is aimed at seeing how able one is to pay bills and debts that are coming due. For example, in analyzing an income property, will it be able to pay those debts coming due in the next year? Included in such debts would be utility bills, real estate taxes, that portion of the mortgage charges payable during the year, operating expenses for the year, etc.

1. *Current Ratio.*

   One of the normal ratios used to test is called the "current ratio." This consists of dividing the current assets by the current liabilities. "Current assets" consist of cash; everything due and collectible within a year, if needed. "Current liabilities" consist of all payments due to be made within the same period.

   There are various *interpretations* of the current ratio. What it should be varies somewhat from industry to industry. However, a widely accepted rule would indicate that the ratio should run about 2:1. Two dollars of current assets for every $1 of current liabilities.

2. *Acid-Test Ratio.*

   This is a more rigid test of liquidity. This is cash on hand, government bonds, and anything that can immediately be turned into cash divided by current liabilities. The rule-of-thumb ratio here is 1:1. In other words, if this test is followed, the project should have enough cash on hand plus cash reserves to cover current expenses for one year.

Leverage

Properties are, in this day and age, rarely owned free and clear by the "owner." If this were not true, there would be little reason for real estate finance or this book. Leverage tests reveal how much of the total financing is put up by the "owner" and how much is put up by his creditors, including the mortgage lender.

1. *Debt-to-Equity Ratio.*

   The total liabilities are divided by the total equity or capital. The rule-of-thumb ratio here will be something between 3:1 and 4:1, ideally. The creditor wants a moderate ratio because the more of his own money the borrower has in the deal, the stronger is his willingness to repay the loan. Conversely, the borrower often wants an extreme ratio because it reduces the amount of his own money that is being risked.

   There are many examples in real estate investment where ratios of 1 to almost 0 are achieved by borrowers. This is usually dangerous to the lender. An exception, of course, would be where the repayment of the loan is guaranteed by some third party in the transaction such as the federal government (FHA and VA) or a financially strong company such as a major chain store or a major oil company.

There are some lenders who are willing to risk entering a high debt-to-equity situation in anticipation of market prices going up. When market prices go up, the owner's equity grows and a more moderate ratio is automatically achieved. Experience has repeatedly shown that this expectation is not always borne out.

2. *Coverage of Fixed Expenses.*

This is a test of how many times net income before income taxes and fixed expenses (gross income minus operating expenses) will cover the fixed expenses. It reveals how low income can drop before the property (or the borrower) will be able to meet the fixed expenses; such as, mortgage loan charges, real estate taxes, and insurance.

Net income after operating expenses is divided by fixed expenses to get this ratio. If the ratio is 1:1, then the net income after operating expenses is just barely able to cover the fixed expenses. This means no profit for the owner. If this situation continues for any time at all, it will obviously affect most owners' willingness to repay unless they have a high cash equity in the project.

In a way this analysis is corollary to the break-even chart discussed earlier. To illustrate the point here, let's use that example again.

To review: 50-unit apartment building . . . fixed expenses = $2,000 per month . . . rents $100 per apartment per month . . . variable expense per apartment per month = $50 . . . assume that all 50 apartments are rented:

Total Gross Income	$ 5,000
Less Variable or Operating Expense	—2,500
Net Before Fixed Expenses	$2,500

Coverage of Fixed Expenses:

$$\frac{\text{Net Before Fixed Expenses}}{\text{Fixed Expenses}} \text{ or } \frac{\$2,500}{\$2,000} = 1.25$$

So, if the net income before fixed expenses dropped more than 25% (or $625), there wouldn't be enough to pay the fixed expenses.

Note: *At first glance, it would appear that the correct answer would be a drop of $500. However, it must be remembered that, as the occupancy of the apartment building drops, so does the variable or operating expenses.*

Activity

Activity tests are designed to reveal just how hard assets are working—how effectively assets are being used.

There are several tests for this, but the most widely used is the "income-to-total asset ratio."

Income-to-Total Assets

This is found by dividing the total income from the property by the total assets. This will reveal how efficiently the assets are working. Activity tests along with leverage tests are keys to determine profitability, as will be seen in the next section. This particular ratio, income-to-total assets, is a key measure in the "du Pont System" of financial control, which will be discussed in a moment.

> **Example:** Suppose property "A" costs a total of $200,000 to create (total assets = $200,000) and it will yield $30,000 per year. Suppose that property "B" costs a total of $200,000 to create (total assets = $200,000) and it will yield $40,000 per year. In which property are the assets working more effectively? Obviously, property "B."

A noncash expense against income by the Internal Revenue Code results in a portion of income being, in a sense, "tax-free." It is actually a device for postponing ordinary income tax charges, and at the same time it transforms them into a capital gain tax to be paid at some future time when the property is sold.

The amount of the "tax shelter" must be calculated on an individual basis, since it obviously must vary with the tax bracket of each owner or investor involved. As a general rule, it amounts to that sum of additional income the taxpayer would have to earn in order to end up with the same amount of "tax-free" income.

To illustrate, let's return to the example of the 50-unit apartment building with $6,000 annual gross income before taxes and an owner who is in the 55% tax bracket. Assume that the depreciation schedule on this building permits him to deduct $2,000 as the noncash depreciation expense. The owner would have had to earn $4,444 under ordinary circumstances, in order to end up with $2,000 "tax-free" or "after taxes." So, the $2,000 tax shelter is the equivalent of $4,444 additional income.

Now, since the $2,000 depreciation allowance lowers his tax base, on which he will have to pay a capital gains tax at the time of a future sale, he might want to be conservative and deduct the amount of that future capital gains tax from the $4,444 in order to arrive at the tax shelter figure.

Whichever way it is done, this tax shelter income should be added to the net spendable cash and principal reduction to arrive at the total return figure.

By dividing this total return figure by the investor's equity (his reasonable present equity—not the amount of his original investment), the investor's yield on his equity can be computed.

This is an important figure, because it shows the yield on the investor's equity and gives him the opportunity to decide whether he should consider alternative investments or allow his equity to remain where it is.

Profitability

Profitability tests are designed to see how much net profit results from the operation relative to income, assets, capital investment, mortgage debts, and so on. There are a variety of ratios and tests that are used to inquire into profitability. Only two of the more common ones will be considered:

1. *Return on Net Worth.*

   This is the ratio of net profit (after taxes) to the net worth or the net investment made in the project. It involves dividing the net profit after taxes by the net worth in the project. This will yield a percentage return on the investment which can then be compared with the return available from other investments of comparable risk.

   Using the 50-unit apartment building again as an example: If it is completely occupied (admittedly, unlikely), the total monthly gross profit = $500. The annual gross profit, before taxes = $6,000. Assume the owner is in a 55% tax bracket and must pay $3,300 in income taxes on this income. His remaining net profit after taxes = $2,700.

   Is this a good return on his equity? It would depend on what his original investment plus appreciation now amounted to and the alternative available.

   If it was $50,000, this might not be too bad for an after-taxes return. If, on the other hand, it was $150,000, there would likely be many other investments that would pay better.

2. *Yield Analysis.*

   This is a form of analysis peculiarly well-suited for determining profitability of real estate projects, because it is relatively easy to compute and takes into consideration the three factors unique in their combination to real estate investment; namely: cash return, equity return, and tax shelter.

It involves dividing the total return by the investor's equity.

The total return is calculated by adding together three component factors: net spendable cash income, principal reduction of mortgage loans, and tax shelter. The first two are generally understood and self-explanatory. The third may require a few words of explanation. The depreciation allowance permitted as a deduction against income allows the investor to have some "tax-free" dollars. These are dollars that are net of any income tax claim. However, we must remember that the more depreciation that is taken, the higher the "profit" will be upon sale of the property. This higher profit will, of course, be subject to capital gains tax. So, the depreciation allowance doesn't yield as many tax-free dollars as it might seem at the outset.

3. *The du Pont System.*

One of the most widely known and accepted methods of judging profitability (and, of instituting controls and improvements in profitability) is the "du Pont System." Its wide use in industry has not filtered down into the field of real estate investment, which is unfortunate.

One of the most important features of the du Pont System is that it not only provides a method of measuring profitability, but also it provides a technique for checking back from the profitability measurement through the various components. This provides an opportunity for checking weaknesses and imposing profit controls where needed in order to improve the profit picture.

An oversimplified version of the du Pont System as applied to real estate income property is:

$$\frac{\text{Gross Rental Income}}{\text{Investment}} \times \frac{\text{Profit Return}}{\text{Gross Rent Income}} = \frac{\text{Profit Return}}{\text{Investment}}$$

Broken down into greater detail, the du Pont System is shown in Figure 10-2 (next page).

CALCULATION-CHECKING SHORTCUTS

When preparing and analyzing various financial reports, one must always guard against errors in calculations. In answer to those who do not regard this as a matter of concern, since the advent of mechanical and electrical calculating machines, it should be pointed out that these are often not available at the time and place where needed. A few old-fashioned tips on calculation-checking shortcuts are, therefore, in order.

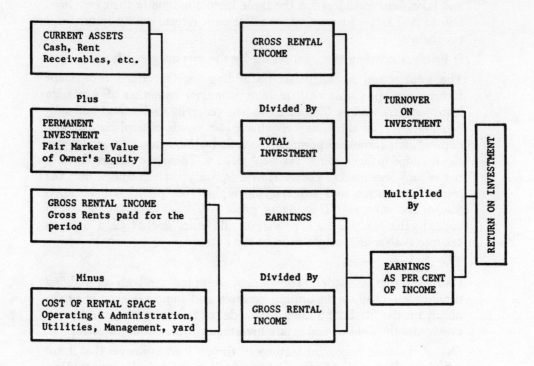

Figure 10-2

Basic Checks

1. *Addition:* Add the figures once again in a different order.
2. *Subtraction:* Add the answer to the smaller of the two numbers of the problem. This should total the larger number of the problem.
3. *Multiplication:* Divide the answer by one of the numbers in the problem. This should equal the other number of the problem.
4. *Division:* Multiply the answer by the divisor and add any remainder. This should equal the dividend (number divided into).

Other Kinds of Checks

1. *Rounded Check on Addition.*

When adding the large numbers, round them off to one or two digits and then add these. The sum should approximate the answer from the first, exact addition.

Example:	73,141	73
	81,332	81
	12,001	12
	63,724	64
	230,198	230

2. *Casting out the Nines Check.*

Add up the digits of each number in the problem (if any of these numbers is a nine, ignore it). *Divide this by nine. Use the remainder as a check number.* Add up the check numbers. Cast out the nines from the total of all the check numbers. The remainder should equal the remainder from casting out the nines from the original answer.

73,141 $7 + 3 + 1 + 4 + 1 = 16 \div 9 = 1 +$ remainder of 7
81,332 $8 + 1 + 3 + 3 + 2 = 17 \div 9 = 1 +$ remainder of 8
12,001 $1 + 2 + 0 + 0 + 1 = 4 \div 9 = 0 +$ remainder of 4
63,724 $6 + 3 + 7 + 2 + 4 = 22 \div 9 = 2 +$ remainder of 4

230,198 $2 + 3 + 0 + 1 + 9 + 8 = 23 \div 9 = 2 +$ rem. of $\textcircled{5}$

$$23 \div 9 =$$
$$2 + \text{rem.} \textcircled{5}$$

To use this method for checking subtraction, multiplication, and division, follow the same procedure in getting check numbers. Then, perform the calculation with the check figures.

3. *Casting out the Elevens on Transposition.*

Casting out the nines does not check on the possibility of a transposition; that is, writing the digits of a number in the wrong order (writing "341" for "143," etc.).

Casting out the elevens provides a check for this addition problem.

Start with the left-hand digit of each number in the original problem. Subtract it from the digit on its right. If the right-hand digit is small, add 11 to it before doing the subtraction. Now, subtract the answer from the next digit on the right (adding 11 if necessary)—and so on, through the entire number. The final answer from the final subtraction is the check number.

Example:

73,141 $(3 + 11) - 7 = 7$; $(1 + 11) - 7 = 5$; $(4 + 11) - 5 = 10$; and, $(1 + 11) - 10 = 2$ (2 is the check number)

81,332 $(1 + 11) - 8 = 4$; $(3 + 11) - 4 = 10$; $(3 + 11) - 10 = 4$; and, $(2 + 11) - 4 = 9$ (9 is the check number)

12,001 $2 - 1 = 1$; $(0 + 11) - 1 = 10$; $(0 + 11) - 10 = 1$;
 $1 - 1 = 0$ (0 is the check number)

63,724 $(3 + 11) - 6 = 8$; $(7 + 11) - 8 = 10$; $(2 + 11) - 10 = 3$;
 $4 - 3 = 1$ (1 is the check number)

We now total the check numbers and cast out the elevens:

$$2 + 9 + 0 + 1 = 12 \div 11 = 1 \text{ with a remainder of } 1$$

We now compare this final remainder of 1 with the check number process applied to the original final answer.

230,198 $3 - 2 = 1$; $(0 + 11) - 1 = 10$; $(1 + 11) - 10 = 2$;
 $9 - 2 = 7$; and, $8 - 7 = 1$

As with casting out the nines, this technique may also be used to check calculations in subtraction, multiplication, and division. Simply get the check numbers and perform the calculation with the check numbers. Let's illustrate with a simple multiplication problem:

Original Problem:

$$
\begin{array}{r}
32{,}157 \\
\times \quad 815 \\
\hline
26{,}207{,}955
\end{array}
$$

Checking:

32,157 $(2 + 11) - 3 = 10$; $(1 + 11) - 10 = 2$; $5 - 2 = 3$; $7 - 3 = 4$ (4 is the check number)

$\times$ 815 $(1 + 11) - 8 = 4$; $5 - 4 = 1$ (1 is the check number)

26,207,955 $6 - 2 = 4$; $(2 + 11) - 4 = 9$; $(0 + 11) - 9 = 2$; $7 - 2 = 5$; $9 - 5 = 4$; $5 - 4 = 1$; $5 - 1 = 4$ (4 is the check number)

Check Problem:

$$
\begin{array}{r}
4 \\
\times \quad 1 \\
\hline
4
\end{array}
$$

POINTS TO KEEP IN MIND

Analysis is the key to sound and profitable investing in real estate.

- *Financial reports as a basis for financial commitment to a real estate project have two major weaknesses: (a) they look backward and not forward; (b) too many people can't really make sense out of them.*

- *Two basic kinds of financial reports are the balance sheet and the operating statement. Both follow the "ALICE" rule for postings.*
- *Additional financial reports of importance are:*

  —Source and Use of Funds Statement—where does it come from and where does it go?

  —Rent Schedule—often puffed or misleading but helpful nevertheless.

  —Inventory—personal property list (if there is any).

  —Break-Even Chart—visual, confusion clearing, and important!
- *Tools of analysis are:*

  —Liquidity Ratios—how much elbowroom if there's trouble?

  —Leverage Ratios—how much profit can you make off the bank's money?

  —Activity Ratios—how are your assets? Lazy? Hardworking? So-so?

  —Profitability—that's what it's all about, isn't it?

··· 11 ···

Effect of Loans
on Net Yield

════════════════════

Borrowing money has a very substantial effect on the net yield of a property. This was discussed in Chapter 4 where the concept of net yield before capital charges and depreciation was developed. This chapter will focus on some of the things that affect net yield.

Interest Expense

The interest expense is 100% deductible in your income tax. In terms of net yield, this does have a certain appeal to some investors because they want to deduct that interest off of their income tax. It may have a bad effect on the net yield of the property if you get a very high loan with high interest payments, but it may have a very good effect on your personal income tax. For every dollar's worth of tax write-off, you may be saving $1.50 in income tax.

Rate of Interest

This will obviously affect the net yield. The higher the rate, the more that you're going to write off as expense. This is what you may not want to do. When you borrow money, be concerned with the rate of interest that you're paying. I don't mean what it says on the face of the note you sign. I don't mean where it says 6% or 6½%. If you take it on that basis, you're forgetting about the four points you're paying on the side. Some of you may not be familiar with the term "points." Points is a synonym for percentage of the loan that you pay as a premium to get the loan at all. You're going to borrow $1,000 at 6% interest and four points. Four per cent of $1,000 is $40. You don't get $1,000, you get $960. But you're paying 6% interest on $1,000. When you figure that out, you don't end up with 6%. It is closer to 9%. Most banks are advertising 4½% car loans, or maybe to 6%. It seems like a good interest rate. You may go in and borrow money to buy a car at 6% interest. The effective rate of interest that you're actually paying will probably turn out to be closer to 14 because of the various ways they work it out. Suppose you were going to borrow $1,000 at 6% interest. You're going to pay it off over a course of one year in equal monthly payments. Now you are actually only borrowing an average of $500 because you're going to go from $1,000 to zero in the course of a year. The average amount of money that you have to use is $500. Still, you're going to pay 6% interest on $1,000 for a year, which is $60. But, you don't have a $1,000 for a year. It ends up you have the average use of $500 a year, and it has cost you $60. You've paid 12% —that is your effective rate of interest.

Leverage

We talked about leverage before. We said that if the property, before depreciation and before capital charges, will yield a return that is higher than the price you have to pay to borrow the money, then it's a good deal. Suppose that you are putting up one-third of the money to buy this land and the bank is putting up two-thirds. The property yields 7%. If you were to pay cash for it, it would yield 7% net. That is 7% before mortgage payments, interest, and depreciation. That means that on your one-third, you're going to get 7%. If you borrow from the bank and pay 8%, you're going to have to pay 1% more for their money. Their money is twice as much as your money, so the yield has been cut by 2%. The return on your investment is now 5%. If you can borrow the money at 6%, that gives you 1% profit on the bank's money. This is twice as much as the profit on your money. Here is a case where you are making 7% on your money plus 2%. That is what is called leverage. In the first case it is negative leverage, from the point of view of the investor. He is being levered down because he has to pay the bank more interest than the property is yielding. It would be called positive leverage if the investor makes money on the bank's money as in the latter case.

Amortization Burden

This is a very important question. Setting aside the question of interest, you have to reduce the principal in your annual or monthly payments on an amortized loan. Decide if the property can afford to carry that burden. An amortized loan has a monthly or quarterly payment program set up so that at the end of the length of the loan it is all paid off. A nonamortized loan may have no payments except interest. Then the principal is paid off in a lump sum at the end of the time.

This is not uncommon with developers. A developer will frequently go in and get an unimproved property loan to buy some acreage that he wants to develop in two or three years. He gets a land loan, sometimes called a land draw. He pays no interest at all for a year. Then he starts paying annual interest payments, and at the end of the three years, he pays off the lump sum of the principal and any interest that has accrued. This enables the builder to begin his project with as little possible carrying charges as he can get away with, while he gets his plans developed, his sales program worked up, and his building permit. Suppose you are making 9% profit on the property, but the whole 9% profit is buried in the buildup of the equity. There is no cash generated. As a matter of fact, you have to pay out $800 a year to cover the taxes because your cash flow isn't enough to pay them. You hope the market doesn't drop while you're building up equity. Can the property carry that amortization burden?

Sliding Scale Amortization. The investor has an advantage in a rising market. You borrow money today that has a certain purchasing power right now. You pay it off over 25 years with dollars that are each year becoming less valuable, as far as purchasing power is concerned. That is one of the biggest advantages of investing in real estate. Borrow as much as the property can afford to carry with reasonable safety. Use that money to build an investment up elsewhere, to pyramid. Of course, the pyramid will collapse if you build it up too fast.

You need to have some liquid reserves. You have to be able to carry property. Be a little conservative. The point is that you're paying off the loan with inflated dollars.

I've long maintained that a more sensible way of paying off mortgages would be on a rising amortization basis. You would borrow the money today, and instead of paying off in level payments, you would pay off in increasingly higher payments each year. Your payments would be low today, and a little bit higher next year, taking into consideration the fact that the purchasing power of the dollar is going down. This would make a much sounder basis for investors.

It would be a sounder basis for banks and savings and loan associations. They could then make their loans of shorter duration because they would pay off faster without strangling the investor. But it seems too complicated, so people will just pay the way they are now doing it for the rest of their lives.

Loan Term

The term of the loan is very important. The longer the loan, the lower the payment. There is a larger payment to be made on a ten-year loan than on a 30-year loan. There are several kinds of loans: conventional loans, leasehold loans, collateral loans, interim loans, and unimproved property loans. Sources of these loans are: national banks and state banks, insurance companies, and savings and loan companies. The savings and loan institutions are federally chartered and state chartered. The main difference between a national bank and a state bank, a federal savings and loan association and a state savings and loan association is that some are chartered by the federal government and some are chartered by the state. There are some minor differences in the amounts that they can lend. Nevertheless, they are pretty well regulated along the same lines.

Conventional Loans. Now take a look at conventional loans. There are two kinds of properties—residential and commercial-industrial. The maximum loan under residential properties is figured in terms of the percentage of the appraisal. National banks can lend 80% of their appraised value. Five financial institutions will appraise the same property for a different amount of money. The amount of their appraisal is all too often determined by how much money they have in the vault on which they are paying 5% interest to the savers. Have you ever figured out what 5% per day on $10 million is? It is a lot of money. Savings and loan associations don't like to have it just sitting there. They want to see it earning more money. They have two kinds of loans. They could get 80% of the appraised value for a maximum of 25 years if the loan is not amortized. State banks go 75%; the term is not limited by statute. It can go as long or as short as they want. On amortized loans, a clause says: "or as provided by the laws of the state in which the company is chartered." This is needed because insurance companies are chartered by different states, and various states have different regulations. The same kind of pattern follows for commercial-industrial properties.

Leasehold Loans. A leasehold loan is a loan that is made on the basis of a lease. Suppose you don't own the land (you are leasing the land) and you want to borrow money to erect a building on it. These loans are pretty difficult to get unless you have a dependable tenant to occupy the building. On a leasehold loan, a national bank can go 66⅔ or two-thirds of the appraised value of the property, "provided that the lease does not expire for at least ten years after the loan matures." So if you wanted a 20-year loan on a piece of property you're leasing to construct a building, you would have to have at least a 30-year loan. Between the time you sign the lease and the time the loan is recorded, plans are drawn, and the permit is issued, a year or two may elapse. So if you obtain a 30-year loan, you may find out that you can only get 18 years. What you need is say a 35-year loan.

Collateral Loans. Collateral loans are loans that are made on things other than real estate, usually on trust deeds or mortgages. If a man owns $50,000 worth of second trust deeds, and he needs some cash, he can go to the bank, use the trust deeds as collateral, and then borrow money on them. That is called a collateral loan. Only banks are permitted to make them. It would be hard to get a bank to make a collateral loan on a second trust deed. The market could change, however.

Unimproved Property Loans. On unimproved property loans or raw land loans, the terms are not quite as good as other loans. The terms recently have improved markedly in the case of banks and savings and loan associations. State banks can now loan 75% for 20 years; they used to be limited to five years.

POINTS TO KEEP IN MIND

Borrowing money against real estate has a substantial effect on what the net yield on your investment will be. Some of the factors to consider are:

- *Interest expense.*
- *Rate of interest.*
- *Leverage.*
- *Amortization burden.*
- *Term of loan.*

Various ways to borrow money against a real estate project are possible including: conventional loans, leasehold loans, collateral loans, and raw land loans.

···12···

The Use of Tables to Build Bigger Profits for You

One of the most helpful tools available to any investor is the one which they shy away from most quickly. That is, the use of mathematical investment tables. The reason for this is that many investors are awed or intimidated by mathematical formulas and the tables that are produced by them. I believe most of us feel these complicated mathematical formulas are really something within the province of the engineer or the statistician. We accept the judgement of these technicians and feel that the whole matter is too complicated for us to understand. We just accept these tables at face value and don't even try to understand them.

The fact of the matter is, it is not important that you understand *how* these tables are calculated. The important thing is that you know how to use the end result—namely, the tables. You don't have to understand the mathematical formula at all. In fact it may even be better if you don't understand it, because then you'll be less concerned with the formula and the working of the formula than you are with the actual investment information resulting from the use of the table. Some people get so caught up in the mystery of employing the formula that they forget what the objective of the whole thing is—namely, to get the highest net profit possible.

The reason that this is all important is that too many investors rely on elementary school mathematics or what seems to be obvious, when, in fact, these mathematics mislead them or "what seems to be obvious" is not obvious at all. As a result, they make investments that are very bad; they do not get a good return on their investment or anywhere near the return that they think they are getting. By the same token, there are people who will sell property that they think is not a good investment because they don't understand what the investment is really bringing them. They will sell a property that is probably a very profitable investment, or trade it for one that is not as good.

Kinds of Tables

There are all kinds of investment tables that are available, but I think we should concentrate on just four. Each of these is really only a variation of one of the others.

1. *Lump Sum or Installments?*

   In real estate investment, you are generally talking about one of two situations, from the point of view of finance. Either you are talking about a lump-sum situation where you want to know something having to do with a lump amount; or, you're concerned with an installment situation, where you want to know something about an amount of money that is paid in installments—in small bits and pieces—over a period of time. So, one of the main factors in a discussion of tables is to decide whether you are talking about a lump sum or an installment situation.

2. *Time Value.*

   The other factor is time. Money has time value. That is to say that a dollar today is worth more than a dollar you will get a year from now. That, in turn, is worth more than a dollar you will get ten years from now.

I think, philosophically (and who cares about that), that part of this relates to the mortality of man. Man realizes that he has a limited amount of time on this Earth and, therefore, time is important to him. Money that he can have in his hand to spend right now is more important to him than money he'll get ten years from now when he might not be around to spend it. It's the old "bird in the hand" philosophy.

The time value of money is expressed in what we call "interest." In other words, whatever time value we think money has we express in a percentage of the amount of money involved and call it interest. Illustrative of this situation is that when you borrow money and have the use of it for a time then you have to pay interest. By the same token, when you let a bank or savings and loan association use your money for a period of time, they must pay interest on it.

The purpose of many tables that you'll be interested in is to figure out for you what this time value of money, or this interest, is worth. Now, there are two ways that you would want to figure interest. One way is from one particular point in time forward to a future time. The other way is the reverse, this would be from a point in time back to an earlier or previous time.

3. *The Two Variables.*

You have, then, the two variables that you're dealing with—either a lump sum or an installment situation; and, you have the time value of money—interest. This chapter will be concerned with four tables. One of the tables will deal with a lump sum and figuring the time value from one point to another point in the future. This type of table will be referred to as a "future lump-sum table." The other table figures the time value of a lump sum of money from some period back to a previous time. This will be designated as a "present table." Lump sums will be dealt with in both cases, but one will be a future table and one will be a present table.

The other variation is the same sort of thing as far as the time matter is concerned, but instead of a lump sum it will be dealing with installment payments—the value of them at some time in the future vs. the value of taking them back to the present.

Lump Sum–Future Table (See Figure 12-1)

Let's begin by considering one of the simpler of the four tables. This is a lump sum–future table. It will tell us what the time value is of a lump sum at some future date. A typical illustration of this kind of problem follows:

Figure 12-1
LUMP SUM–FUTURE TABLE *

Years	2½%	3%	3½%	4%	4½%	5%	6%
1	1.0250	1.0300	1.0350	1.0400	1.0450	1.0500	1.0600
2	1.0506	1.0609	1.0712	1.0816	1.0920	1.1025	1.1236
3	1.0769	1.0927	1.1087	1.1249	1.1412	1.1576	1.1910
4	1.1038	1.1255	1.1475	1.1699	1.1925	1.2155	1.2625
5	1.1314	1.1593	1.1877	1.2167	1.2462	1.2763	1.3382
6	1.1597	1.1941	1.2293	1.2653	1.3023	1.3401	1.4185
7	1.1887	1.2299	1.2723	1.3159	1.3609	1.4071	1.5036
8	1.2184	1.2668	1.3168	1.3686	1.4221	1.4775	1.5938
9	1.2489	1.3048	1.3629	1.4233	1.4861	1.5513	1.6895
10	1.2801	1.3439	1.4106	1.4802	1.5530	1.6289	1.7908
11	1.3121	1.3842	1.4600	1.5395	1.6229	1.7103	1.8983
12	1.3449	1.4258	1.5111	1.6010	1.6959	1.7959	2.0122
13	1.3785	1.4685	1.5640	1.6651	1.7722	1.8856	2.1329
14	1.4130	1.5126	1.6187	1.7317	1.8519	1.9799	2.2609
15	1.4483	1.5580	1.6753	1.8009	1.9353	2.0789	2.3966
16	1.4845	1.6047	1.7340	1.8730	2.0224	2.1829	2.5404
17	1.5216	1.6528	1.7947	1.9479	2.1134	2.2920	2.6928
18	1.5597	1.7024	1.8575	2.0258	2.2085	2.4066	2.8543
19	1.5986	1.7535	1.9225	2.1068	2.3079	2.5269	3.0256
20	1.6386	1.8061	1.9898	2.1911	2.4117	2.6533	3.2071
21	1.6796	1.8603	2.0594	2.2788	2.5202	2.7860	3.3996
22	1.7216	1.9161	2.1315	2.3699	2.6337	2.9253	3.6035
23	1.7646	1.9736	2.2061	2.4647	2.7522	3.0715	3.8197
24	1.8087	2.0328	2.2833	2.5633	2.8760	3.2251	4.0489
25	1.8539	2.0938	2.3632	2.6658	3.0054	3.3864	4.2919
26	1.9003	2.1566	2.4460	2.7725	3.1407	3.5557	4.5494
27	1.9478	2.2213	2.5316	2.8834	3.2820	3.7335	4.8223
28	1.9965	2.2879	2.6202	2.9987	3.4297	3.9201	5.1117
29	2.0464	2.3566	2.7119	3.1187	3.5840	4.1161	5.4184
30	2.0976	2.4273	2.8068	3.2434	3.7453	4.3219	5.7435
31	2.1500	2.5001	2.9050	3.3731	3.9139	4.5380	6.0881
32	2.2038	2.5751	3.0067	3.5081	4.0900	4.7649	6.4534
33	2.2589	2.6523	3.1119	3.6484	4.2740	5.0032	6.8406
34	2.3153	2.7319	3.2209	3.7943	4.4664	5.2533	7.2510
35	2.3732	2.8139	3.3336	3.9461	4.6673	5.5160	7.6861
36	2.4325	2.8983	3.4503	4.1039	4.8774	5.7918	8.1473
37	2.4933	2.9852	3.5710	4.2681	5.0969	6.0814	8.6361
38	2.5557	3.0748	3.6960	4.4388	5.3262	6.3855	9.1543
39	2.6196	3.1670	3.8254	4.6164	5.5659	6.7048	9.7035
40	2.6851	3.2620	3.9593	4.8010	5.8164	7.0400	10.2857
41	2.7522	3.3599	4.0978	4.9931	6.0781	7.3920	10.9029
42	2.8210	3.4607	4.2413	5.1928	6.3516	7.7616	11.5570
43	2.8915	3.5645	4.3897	5.4005	6.6374	8.1497	12.2505
44	2.9638	3.6715	4.5433	5.6165	6.9361	8.5571	12.9855
45	3.0379	3.7816	4.7024	5.8412	7.2482	8.9850	13.7646
46	3.1139	3.8950	4.8669	6.0748	7.5744	9.4343	14.5905
47	3.1917	4.0119	5.0373	6.3178	7.9153	9.9060	15.4659
48	3.2715	4.1323	5.2136	6.5705	8.2715	10.4013	16.3939
49	3.3533	4.2562	5.3961	6.8333	8.6437	10.9213	17.3775
50	3.4371	4.3839	5.5849	7.1067	9.0326	11.4674	18.4202

---

* Used by permission of the American Institute of Real Estate Appraisers.

Problem Number 1

You deposit $1,000 in a savings and loan account that pays 5% interest, compounded annually. If you put $1,000 in today, how much interest will this money have earned one year in the future? In other words, what is $1,000 today going to grow to at 5% interest in one year? This is a fairly simple problem, and I'm sure you already know the answer. Five per cent for one year on $1,000 is $50, so the future value of $1,000 one year from today with an interest rate of 5% is $1,050. Obviously, if the rate of interest was different, or if the time was different, the figure would change—because $1,000 at 5% two years from now would be $1,100, assuming you did not compound the interest. If you did compound the interest—that is to say, figured it every year; paid interest on the interest so that the first year you're paying 5% on $1,050 —then, the value in the future (two years in the future) would be $1,102.50.

Problem Number 2

Suppose you bought a piece of property in 1930 for $10,000. This year someone comes along and wants to buy it from you. You tell them that you will sell it for the same price you paid for it in 1930, plus 6% interest on the money that you have had invested. Now, you've had $10,000 invested from 1930 to the present. Let's say this covers a 40-year period, and you want 6% return at simple interest. At 6% a year on $10,000, that would be $600 per year for 40 years or $24,000 for the interest, plus your original investment of $10,000. So, you would want $34,000.

Now there are many people who look at a problem like this and do not understand that what they want to use is a future table, because they are working toward a present date. What they don't understand is that in this particular kind of problem they are working from a point in time (in the particular instance I make reference to here, the point in time is 1930) and they are moving into the future from that time to the present year. So, you would be using this kind of a future table and dealing again with a lump sum. A word of caution: I said the return would be figured on the basis of simple interest. That's to make the example easier for us to talk about because it becomes very clear what 6% of $10,000 is every year. Obviously, in actual life, you would be doing it at compound interest, since that's the way we do things nowadays and the real figure would not be $24,000 in interest but rather $92,857.

Here, you have an example of such a future table. Notice at the very beginning that this is for $1, since obviously it is impossible to know what amount of money you are talking about in every specific case. Therefore, by simply setting up the table in terms of $1, you can multiply the index number that you will find in the table by the number of dollars you're dealing with. If you will notice, the table has four important parts to it that concern you.

The first part is the heading. Be sure you look at the heading of any table before you use it, so that you know exactly what it is the table is going to tell you. For this particular table the heading is the future value of $1 (lump sum), so that we know that we are talking about a lump sum situation and not installments. The second part of the table that is important to you is the column on the extreme left-hand side. This gives you the number of years in the future. You'll see that it is headed years and that it counts down from 1 through 50. Across the top is the third thing that should concern you, and that gives you the heading of each of the other columns in terms of what you're thinking of about the time value of the money that you want to know about. This is the interest rate; so this runs from 2½ % through 6%. The fourth thing that is important to you is the body of the table, where the index or key numbers are, that you can use to apply to your particular problem. Thus, by simply going down the left-hand column (the one with the years in it) to the year that you're interested in and then running your eye or finger across to the right until you get under the interest figure that concerns you, you will find the index or key number. Now, if you take this number and multiply it by the number of dollars involved in your investment, you will then get the exact compound interest. To illustrate how this works, study the following example. Examples are based on the assumption that the interest is not withdrawn each time it is earned, but is left to compound.

Example Number 1

Suppose you were to leave $15,000 in a savings account that earned 4% compounded annually. How much would have accumulated, compounded that way, in ten years? Well, you look at the table, run your eye or finger down the year column until you get to ten for ten years, and then read across to the column headed 4%—and the factor you will find is 1.4802. Multiply this times your investment of $15,000 and the answer is $22,203.

Example Number 2

Let's say you bought a lot for $12,300, 15 years ago. You want to earn 6% on your investment. What should you sell it for today? We are going to assume here that you have been able to earn some income from this lot to offset the cost of carrying it—to pay for the taxes. If you haven't, of course, you want to figure that cost, too, and whatever else you've had to pay, if there was insurance or anything of that sort.

But, let's just look at it from the point of view of the $12,300 that you invested 15 years ago. Now, here is an example of the situation that I mentioned previously; namely, that too frequently people think when you're talking about a future table you're talking about a situation that has to be in the future from today. That isn't the case at all. The case is that it is in the future from the point of time from which you're starting. So, if you start 15 years ago when you bought this lot and you work forward to the future, you are getting to today (obviously) but you're still using a future table because you're starting from one point in time and moving forward.

So, you look at the table for that. (It is assumed that you want to get 6% on your money.) In this instance, you run down the outside column until you get to the fifteenth year, then read across to the 6% column, and the factor you'll get from the table is 2.3966. If you multiply that times $12,300, the answer you'll get is $29,478. So, you should sell that lot today for $29,478 if you want to earn 6% return on your investment over this period of time.

Example Number 3

Here is another kind of problem that you can use the table for by working backwards. Suppose you want to find out the answer to the following question. How long will it take to double your money on a lot purchased for $6,500 if the rate of interest is 5%? Well, it really doesn't make any difference how much your investment is—how many dollars you've got in it—because all you're looking for now is a factor in the table that will double your money. So, what you're looking for is a factor of 2.000.

What you do in this case is look across the top of the table to the column that's headed 5%, and then you run your finger down the index or key numbers until you find a number 2.000 or as close to it as you can. In this case, the number for the fourteenth year is 1.9799 which is very close, and the number for 15 years is 2.0789 which is a little bit more than you want. So, if you calculate the difference or, as some people say—interpolate—you find out that 2.000 is about 3/10ths of the difference between 1.9799 and 2.0789, so the exact answer in this case would be it takes 14.3 years to double your money at 5%. Or, you could just round it off and say it takes a little over 14 years to double your money at 5%.

Future Value–Installment Table (See Figure 12-2)

Now, you go into a variation on the last table mentioned. Again, you are looking at the future value of money from the point in time that you're considering, but this time you are looking at it as a series of installment payments rather than one lump-sum payment. In other words, instead of asking what is $10,000 invested in 1930 worth at 6% interest this year, you're talking about a series of payments that are made over this same period of time (and you have to compound the interest for varying periods).

Let's take, for example, a situation where you say, "If I deposit $1,000 a year in a savings account at 5% interest, how much will this all total at the end of ten years?" If you assume that at the beginning of each year, you are going to deposit $1,000 in a savings account and that the savings account is going to earn 5% every year for the next ten years, you want to know how much that will total up to. Now, here is where the problem becomes complicated. $1,000 in the bank for one year at 5% will earn, obviously, $50. The next year that same $1,000, having grown to $1,050, will have to be figured at 5% on $1,050 plus 5% on the second $1,000. So, what it amounts to is that you have $1,000 that is in there for the entire ten years, a second $1,000 that is in there for nine years, a third that is in there for eight years, and so on until you reach the end of the ten-year period.

Here, again, you have a simple table that you can refer to. Just like the previous one, look at the left-hand column, find the number of years you want, and read across on that line to get the interest rate involved. That gives you an index or key figure and you multiply that figure times the number of dollars involved. That will tell you what the total amount is worth in the future.

Now, remember, in the use of this table and the example, that you're concerned with a situation where the amount of the installment remains the same each time and the interest rate remains constant throughout the period of time. Obviously, if the interest rate changes or if the installments are of varying amounts, then this table is useless to you. In that case, you'll have to figure it out by using the lump-sum table, adding up for each case, and then adding them all together to get the sum total. Following is an example.

Example Number 1

Suppose you deposit $5,000 a year at 4% compound interest. How much will it be in 18 years? You are making an identical deposit of $5,000

Figure 12-2
FUTURE VALUE—INSTALLMENT TABLE *

Years	2½%	3%	3½%	4%	4½%	6%
1	1.0250	1.0300	1.0350	1.0400	1.0450	1.0600
2	2.0756	2.0909	2.1062	2.1216	2.1370	2.1836
3	3.1525	3.1836	3.2149	3.2465	3.2782	3.3746
4	4.2563	4.3091	4.3625	4.4163	4.4707	4.6371
5	5.3877	5.4684	5.5502	5.6330	5.7169	5.9753
6	6.5474	6.6625	6.7794	6.8983	7.0192	7.3938
7	7.7361	7.8923	8.0517	8.2142	8.3800	8.8975
8	8.9545	9.1591	9.3685	9.5828	9.8021	10.4913
9	10.2034	10.4639	10.7314	11.0061	11.2882	12.1808
10	11.4835	11.8078	12.1420	12.4864	12.8412	13.9716
11	12.7956	13.1920	13.6020	14.0258	14.4640	15.8699
12	14.1404	14.6178	15.1130	15.6268	16.1599	17.8821
13	15.5190	16.0863	16.6770	17.2919	17.9321	20.0151
14	16.9319	17.5989	18.2957	19.0236	19.7841	22.2760
15	18.3802	19.1569	19.9710	20.8245	21.7193	24.6725
16	19.8647	20.7616	21.7050	22.6975	23.7417	27.2129
17	21.3863	22.4144	23.4997	24.6454	25.8551	29.9057
18	22.9460	24.1169	25.3572	26.6712	28.0636	32.7600
19	24.5446	25.8704	27.2797	28.7781	30.3714	35.7856
20	26.1833	27.6765	29.2695	30.9692	32.7831	38.9927
21	27.8629	29.5368	31.3289	33.2480	35.3034	42.3923
22	29.5844	31.4529	33.4604	35.6179	37.9370	45.9958
23	31.3490	33.4265	35.6665	38.0826	40.6892	49.8156
24	33.1578	35.4593	37.9499	40.6459	43.5652	53.8645
25	35.0117	37.5530	40.3131	43.3117	46.5706	58.1564
26	36.9120	39.7096	42.7591	46.0842	49.7113	62.7058
27	38.8598	41.9309	45.2906	48.9676	52.9933	67.5281
28	40.8563	44.2189	47.9108	51.9663	56.4230	72.6398
29	42.9027	46.5754	50.6227	55.0849	60.0071	78.0582
30	45.0003	49.0027	53.4295	58.3283	63.7524	83.8017
31	47.1503	51.5028	56.3345	61.7015	67.6662	89.8898
32	49.3540	54.0778	59.3412	65.2095	71.7562	96.3432
33	51.6129	56.7302	62.4531	68.8579	76.0303	103.1838
34	53.9282	59.4621	65.6740	72.6522	80.4966	110.4348
35	56.3014	62.2759	69.0076	76.5983	85.1640	118.1209
36	58.7339	65.1742	72.4579	80.7022	90.0413	126.2681
37	61.2273	68.1594	76.0289	84.9703	95.1382	134.9042
38	63.7830	71.2342	79.7249	89.4091	100.4644	144.0585
39	66.4026	74.4013	83.5503	94.0255	106.0303	153.7620
40	69.0876	77.6633	87.5095	98.8265	111.8467	164.0477
41	71.8398	81.0232	91.6074	103.8196	117.9248	174.9505
42	74.6608	84.4839	95.8486	109.0124	124.2764	186.5076
43	77.5523	88.0484	100.2383	114.4129	130.9138	198.7580
44	80.5161	91.7199	104.7817	120.0294	137.8500	211.7435
45	83.5540	95.5015	109.4840	125.8706	145.0982	225.5081
46	86.6679	99.3965	114.3510	131.9454	152.6726	240.0986
47	89.8596	103.4084	119.3882	138.2632	160.5879	255.5645
48	93.1311	107.5406	124.6018	144.8337	168.8594	271.9584
49	96.4843	111.7969	129.9979	151.6671	177.5030	289.3359
50	99.9215	116.1808	135.5828	158.7738	186.5357	307.7561

* Used by permission of the American Institute of Real Estate Appraisers.

at the beginning of every year and you're letting it compound—not taking any of the interest out. How much will that grow to in 18 years? You find the year column on the table, go down to the eighteenth year, read across to 4%, and the factor there is 26.6712. Multiply that times your constant installment of $5,000 and you get an answer of $133,356.

Present Value–Lump-Sum Table (See Figure 12-3)

Here is another kind of variation of the types of tables discussed. This is a table that deals with a lump sum just like the first table studied. However, this one, instead of moving from a point in time forward to the future, moves from a point in time backward—usually to the present time, but not necessarily. Its most common usage is in connection with the present time. Therefore it is called a present value table. The use of this is fairly easy to see.

What you're trying to do here is find out what the value is today of a lump sum of money to be paid at some later time. This is, in essence, taking that lump sum to be paid later and discounting it, or subtracting from it the compound interest it would earn during that time from the present until the time when it is to be paid. By this process of discounting, we find out what its value is today.

For example, suppose someone says to you, "I will promise to pay you $1,000 one year from now. How much money will you give me today in exchange for that promise?" That means you are going to have to forego the use of that $1,000 for one year, during which time a lot of things can happen. But, at any rate, taking into consideration the time value of money, what is it worth to you to go without that $1,000 for one year? You have to think in terms of the time value of money as interest. Let's say that you decide the time value of money to you is 5% per year. You then say the interest that $1,000 could earn in one year at 5% would be $50. Therefore, if you promise to pay me $1,000 one year from today, I will give you $950 today. This is the $1,000 less the interest which it would have earned in that year.

Now of course it could be more or less than $50, depending on how frequently you compound it and so on. It has been expressed here merely as 5% at simple interest, so that it is an-easy-to-see example. However, everything is figured at compound interest in the investment world. Therefore, it would be more proper for you to calculate this on a compound interest basis. Once again, you have the easy-to-use tool of the table. If you look at the table shown here, following down the left-hand column to the line indicating the year at which this debt will be paid

Figure 12-3
PRESENT VALUE–LUMP-SUM TABLE *

Years	8%	9%	10%	11%	12%	13%	14%	15%
1	.9259	.9174	.9091	.9009	.8929	.8850	.8772	.8696
2	.8573	.8417	.8264	.8116	.7972	.7831	.7695	.7561
3	.7938	.7722	.7513	.7312	.7118	.6930	.6750	.6575
4	.7350	.7084	.6830	.6587	.6355	.6133	.5921	.5718
5	.6806	.6499	.6209	.5935	.5674	.5428	.5194	.4972
6	.6302	.5963	.5645	.5346	.5066	.4803	.4556	.4323
7	.5835	.5470	.5132	.4816	.4523	.4250	.3996	.3759
8	.5403	.5019	.4665	.4339	.4039	.3762	.3506	.3269
9	.5002	.4604	.4241	.3909	.3606	.3329	.3075	.2843
10	.4632	.4224	.3855	.3522	.3220	.2946	.2697	.2472
11	.4289	.3875	.3505	.3173	.2875	.2607	.2366	.2149
12	.3971	.3555	.3186	.2858	.2567	.2307	.2075	.1869
13	.3677	.3262	.2897	.2575	.2292	.2042	.1821	.1625
14	.3405	.2992	.2633	.2320	.2046	.1807	.1597	.1413
15	.3152	.2745	.2394	.2090	.1827	.1599	.1401	.1229
16	.2919	.2519	.2176	.1883	.1631	.1415	.1229	.1069
17	.2703	.2311	.1978	.1696	.1456	.1252	.1078	.0929
18	.2502	.2120	.1799	.1528	.1300	.1108	.0946	.0808
19	.2317	.1945	.1635	.1377	.1161	.0981	.0829	.0703
20	.2145	.1784	.1486	.1240	.1037	.0868	.0728	.0611
21	.1987	.1637	.1351	.1117	.0925	.0768	.0638	.0531
22	.1839	.1502	.1228	.1007	.0826	.0680	.0560	.0462
23	.1703	.1378	.1117	.0907	.0738	.0601	.0491	.0402
24	.1577	.1264	.1015	.0817	.0659	.0532	.0431	.0349
25	.1460	.1160	.0923	.0736	.0588	.0471	.0378	.0304
26	.1352	.1064	.0839	.0663	.0525	.0417	.0331	.0264
27	.1252	.0976	.0763	.0597	.0469	.0369	.0291	.0230
28	.1159	.0895	.0693	.0538	.0419	.0326	.0255	.0200
29	.1073	.0822	.0630	.0485	.0374	.0289	.0224	.0174
30	.0994	.0754	.0573	.0437	.0334	.0256	.0196	.0151
31	.0920	.0691	.0521	.0394	.0298	.0226	.0172	.0131
32	.0852	.0634	.0474	.0354	.0266	.0200	.0151	.0114
33	.0789	.0582	.0431	.0319	.0238	.0177	.0132	.0099
34	.0730	.0534	.0391	.0288	.0212	.0157	.0116	.0086
35	.0676	.0490	.0356	.0259	.0189	.0139	.0102	.0075
36	.0626	.0449	.0323	.0234	.0169	.0123	.0089	.0065
37	.0580	.0412	.0294	.0210	.0151	.0109	.0078	.0057
38	.0537	.0378	.0267	.0189	.0135	.0096	.0069	.0049
39	.0497	.0347	.0243	.0171	.0120	.0085	.0060	.0043
40	.0460	.0318	.0221	.0154	.0107	.0075	.0053	.0037
41	.0426	.0292	.0201	.0139	.0096	.0067	.0046	.0032
42	.0395	.0268	.0183	.0125	.0086	.0059	.0041	.0028
43	.0365	.0246	.0166	.0112	.0076	.0052	.0036	.0025
44	.0338	.0225	.0151	.0101	.0068	.0046	.0031	.0021
45	.0313	.0207	.0137	.0091	.0061	.0041	.0027	.0019
46	.0290	.0190	.0125	.0082	.0054	.0036	.0024	.0016
47	.0269	.0174	.0113	.0074	.0049	.0032	.0021	.0014
48	.0249	.0160	.0103	.0067	.0043	.0028	.0019	.0012
49	.0230	.0147	.0094	.0060	.0039	.0025	.0016	.0011
50	.0213	.0134	.0085	.0054	.0035	.0022	.0014	.0009

* Used by permission of the American Institute of Real Estate Appraisers.

to you, and then follow the line across to the column headed by the interest rate you want to earn on your money, that will give you a factor —the factor for $1. Multiply that factor (or key or index number) by the number of dollars you are talking about, and that will give you the present value of the amount of money that will be paid to you at a future date. To illustrate, let's use some examples.

Example Number 1

Suppose that someone comes to you with a second mortgage payable in a lump sum two years from now in the amount of $4,500. He wants to sell it to you and you say, "Well, under the terms of this second mortgage, I will receive $4,500 in two years." Now, suppose you want to earn 8% interest on your money. You simply look down the left-hand column of the table to number two—for two years—and then read across to the line which says 8%. This will give you your index or key number which, in this particular case, is .8573. If you multiply .8573 times the $4,500, you will see that the amount of money you should pay for this mortgage, in order to earn 8% compounded annually, is $3,857.85.

Example Number 2

Suppose you make a ground lease with a tenant and, as part of the terms of the ground lease, the building that he puts on the property is to become yours at the end of the lease. In other words, the improvements on the property revert to you. Let's say, for the purpose of discussion, that the value of the improvements at the time they revert to you will be $23,-000. Let's further assume that the lease is 50 years long and that you, or any other investor, would discount anything of this sort at a rate of 8%— you want an 8% return on your investment. So what is this building worth to you today if it's worth $23,000 in 50 years—what is the discounted value of 8% of that building *today?*

Well, here again, you go to the present value of a lump sum table. You run down the column of the years to the 50th year, read across, and find under 8% that the factor or index number is .0213. If you multiply that figure times $23,000, you find out that the building's value today is $489.90. This is information that would be valuable to you either as owner of the property or seller—if you are going to sell the property with the reversion right on it, or if you are going to buy the property. A man is going to sell you the right to a building 50 years from now which will be worth $23,000, so how much should you pay him today? Well, as shown, you should pay him no more than $489.90, if you expect to earn 8% per annum, compounded, on your money. This is the kind of information that these tables can give you and this is why they are such a very important tool to know how to use. Let's try one more example to illustrate another kind of situation. One that is, incidentally, not too uncommon.

Example Number 3

Here is a situation where someone wishes to give their property to someone else but retain a life estate in the property. This is a device that is sometimes used by parents who want to avoid saddling their children with inheritance taxes, so they give some of their property to a child as a gift. In addition to that, however, they wisely don't trust their children to the point where they want to live in a house that is completely owned by them, so they retain a life estate in this property. This gives them the title to the property as long as they live, and, then, at their death, it automatically passes to the person to whom the gift was made originally. The person who gets the title to the property at death has the reversion, or the reversionary right, to the property. Well, lots of times the person who holds this reversionary right doesn't want to sit around and wait for the grantor of the gift to die. They want to convert this reversionary right into cash. So, the question is, "How much is that reversionary right worth?" Well, the first thing you have to establish is when is the title of the property going to pass to the person holding the reversion? For this, the usual technique is to consult a table of life expectancy, or a mortality table, on which to make your calculations. Let's say, for the purpose of our discussion, that the person who holds the life estate in the property—the one who has made the gift to the child, or someone else, of the reversionary right—has a life expectancy of 15 years from today. Let's also assume that 10% minimum will be earned on any investment and that at the time the property passes to the holder of the reversionary right (namely, 15 years from now) the property will be worth $20,000. So, the question really is, "What is a lump sum of $20,000, to be paid in 15 years, worth if it is discounted at the rate of 10% interest?"

Here again, you go to the table, run your eye down the first column to 15 years, and read across until you get to the column that's headed 10%. This gives you a key factor or index figure of .2394. Now multiply this figure times the $20,000, which gives you $4,788. So, if someone wanted to sell you the reversionary right, or if you, yourself, wanted to sell the reversionary right of a property, under the circumstances just described, it should be worth $4,788.

Now, let's go on to the final table in this group of four that is of concern here.

Present Value—Installment Table (See Figure 12-4)

This table is used a great deal in the sale of leasehold interests and other types of transactions that involve installment payments. It is important at the beginning that you understand that when you're talking about installment payments, you cannot use this table unless you're dealing with equal payments. Each payment must be equal, otherwise the table can't handle it. What this table will tell you is the present value of the right to receive a series of installment payments over a period of time, and it is a variation of the second table discussed in this chapter, which talked about the future value of installment payments. So, what you really do here is take, in essence, a sum of many different calculations out of the third table—the present worth of a lump sum. For example, this can be useful if you are talking about an income from an apartment house of $15,300 a year; you assume that this will continue for 25 years, and you want to know what the present value of that kind of a series of income payments is. Now obviously, there are some if's, and's, and but's in this kind of an example, such as how do you know you're going to get $15,300 every year for the 25 years, and so on? However, let's ignore these for the purpose of this example—but don't forget them. I say ignore them just for the purpose of the example, but keep them in the back of your head—for they've got to be equal payments each year and then maybe they're just an estimate. Maybe you're just estimating that you're going to get $15,300 a year from this apartment building every year for 25 years.

Now, one way you could figure out what it is worth today is to go to the third table and ask what the present value of a lump sum of $15,300 is that will be received in one year from now and then add to that what the present value of a lump sum to be received two years from now is, and in three years, four years, and five years—so on, down the line. However, that has already been figured out for you in this particular table. What you do is simply go down the column of years to 25 and read across to whatever rate of interest you think is appropriate for you—and appropriate for the marketplace. In this case, I'm going to use 8% for my example, and you will get a key number of 10.675. If you multiply this by the $15,300, it will tell you that the present value of getting $15,300 a year, every year, for 25 years, figuring an 8% return on your investment, is $163,327.50. Now, if you'd like to do the same thing by the long method with the lump-sum table (the third table) and add them all up, you

Figure 12-4
PRESENT VALUE–INSTALLMENT TABLE *

Years	Speculative Interest Rates							
	6½%	7%	7½%	8%	9%	10%	11%	12%
1	0.939	0.935	0.930	0.926	0.917	0.909	0.901	0.893
2	1.821	1.808	1.796	1.783	1.759	1.736	1.713	1.690
3	2.648	2.624	2.600	2.577	2.531	2.487	2.444	2.402
4	3.426	3.387	3.349	3.312	3.240	3.170	3.102	3.037
5	4.156	4.100	4.046	3.993	3.890	3.791	3.696	3.605
6	4.841	4.766	4.694	4.623	4.486	4.355	4.231	4.111
7	5.485	5.389	5.297	5.206	5.033	4.868	4.712	4.564
8	6.089	5.971	5.857	5.747	5.535	5.335	5.146	4.968
9	6.656	6.515	6.379	6.247	5.995	5.759	5.537	5.328
10	7.189	7.024	6.864	6.710	6.418	6.145	5.889	5.650
11	7.689	7.499	7.315	7.139	6.805	6.495	6.206	5.938
12	8.159	7.943	7.735	7.536	7.161	6.814	6.492	6.194
13	8.600	8.358	8.126	7.904	7.487	7.103	6.750	6.424
14	9.014	8.745	8.489	8.244	7.786	7.367	6.982	6.628
15	9.403	9.108	8.827	8.559	8.061	7.606	7.191	6.811
16	9.768	9.447	9.142	8.851	8.313	7.824	7.379	6.974
17	10.110	9.763	9.434	9.122	8.544	8.022	7.549	7.120
18	10.432	10.059	9.706	9.372	8.756	8.201	7.702	7.250
19	10.735	10.336	9.959	9.604	8.950	8.365	7.839	7.366
20	11.019	10.594	10.194	9.818	9.128	8.514	7.963	7.469
21	11.285	10.835	10.413	10.017	9.292	8.649	8.075	7.562
22	11.535	11.061	10.617	10.201	9.442	8.772	8.176	7.645
23	11.770	11.272	10.807	10.371	9.580	8.883	8.266	7.718
24	11.991	11.469	10.983	10.529	9.707	8.985	8.348	7.784
25	12.198	11.654	11.147	10.675	9.823	9.077	8.422	7.843
26	12.392	11.826	11.299	10.810	9.929	9.161	8.488	7.896
27	12.575	11.987	11.441	10.935	10.026	9.237	8.548	7.943
28	12.746	12.137	11.573	11.051	10.116	9.307	8.602	7.984
29	12.907	12.278	11.696	11.158	10.198	9.370	8.650	8.022
30	13.059	12.409	11.810	11.258	10.274	9.427	8.694	8.055
31	13.201	12.532	11.917	11.350	10.343	9.479	8.733	8.085
32	13.334	12.647	12.015	11.435	10.406	9.526	8.769	8.112
33	13.459	12.754	12.107	11.514	10.464	9.569	8.801	8.135
34	13.577	12.854	12.193	11.587	10.518	9.609	8.829	8.157
35	13.687	12.948	12.272	11.655	10.567	9.644	8.855	8.176
36	13.791	13.035	12.347	11.717	10.612	9.676	8.879	8.193
37	13.888	13.117	12.415	11.775	10.653	9.706	8.900	8.207
38	13.979	13.193	12.479	11.829	10.691	9.733	8.919	8.221
39	14.065	13.265	12.539	11.879	10.726	9.757	8.936	8.233
40	14.145	13.332	12.594	11.925	10.757	9.779	8.951	8.244
41	14.221	13.394	12.646	11.967	10.786	9.799	8.965	8.253
42	14.292	13.452	12.694	12.007	10.813	9.817	8.977	8.262
43	14.359	13.507	12.738	12.043	10.838	9.834	8.989	8.270
44	14.421	13.558	12.780	12.077	10.861	9.849	8.999	8.276
45	14.480	13.605	12.819	12.108	10.881	9.863	9.008	8.283
46	14.535	13.650	12.855	12.137	10.900	9.875	9.016	8.288
47	14.587	13.692	12.888	12.164	10.918	9.887	9.024	8.293
48	14.636	13.730	12.919	12.189	10.933	9.897	9.030	8.297
49	14.682	13.767	12.948	12.212	10.948	9.906	9.036	8.301
50	14.724	13.801	12.975	12.233	10.962	9.915	9.042	8.305

* Used by permission of the American Institute of Real Estate Appraisers.

will find that—within a penny or two—it will come out to the same figure: namely, $163,327.50.

Now, this table has many uses that I think should be immediately evident to you. For example, suppose that you are contemplating buying a mortgage—one that pays so much per year. One of the things you should understand is that it must be equal payments every year. You want to know how much you should pay for that mortgage in order to amass the kind of interest you want to earn. It is also helpful on leases, as has been indicated, and on any other kind of installment payments on which you want to figure today's value.

Some Random Thoughts About the Use of Tables

So you see that the use of tables is something that every investor should learn. These kinds of tables are available at most good bookstores and they are invaluable aids in calculating what you are really getting when you buy or what you are really selling when you sell. They cut down a great deal on the "pencil on the back of an old envelope" work, so I commend any sensible set of tables to your attention as an excellent investment—before you make any really important investments. One little trick that I might mention to you before we leave the matter of tables is that, while we've been talking about the left-hand column of these tables being the number of years, it could just as well be used for example, for semiannual, or quarterly, or even monthly situations. But, you must remember when you do this, that you have to adjust the interest rate at the top of the column. For example, if you're talking about doing something on a quarterly basis, and you want to know what the present value is of an installment payment that goes at the rate of $100 per quarter for a total of five years, you could look down the years column. But, instead of looking at five years, you should look at four installments per year times five years, which equals 20 installments. So you would go down to the twentieth line and then read across to the correct interest rate. Now remember that this is interest rate per annum in that quarter. So, if you're talking about an interest rate of 26% per year, then you'd have to take one-quarter of that and look under the 6½ % column. So, your factor there would be 11.019 times the quarterly payment—11.019 which is on the twentieth period line under 6½ %.

In any event, the tables are an extremely valuable addition to your library and most important for guiding you on investments.

POINTS TO KEEP IN MIND

Real estate finance and mathematical tables can give you quick answers with a minimum of mathematical effort or knowledge. They often hold the key to profit for your investment.

All the tables considered in this chapter are based on two variables:

- *Lump sums vs. installments.*
- *The time value of money.*

This means you are primarily concerned with four basic tables:

- *Future Value–Lump-Sum Table. (A lump sum to be paid at some time in the future is worth how much at the payoff date?)*
- *Future Value–Installment Table. (A series of payments, or installments, to be paid in the future is worth how much?)*
- *Present Value–Lump-Sum Table. (What is the present value of a lump sum due to be paid in the future?)*
- *Present Value–Installment Table. (What is the present value of a series of payments, or installments, to be paid in the future?)*

V

SPECIFIC TYPES OF
REAL ESTATE INVESTMENTS

···13···

Raw Land
as an Investment

The first thing to do in buying raw land is decide what your aim is as an investor. Usually people who buy raw land or acreage have appreciation in mind. They think the land is going to just increase in value. Then, they can sell it for a capital gain. They are not looking for a tax shelter or for income. The kind of income you can get from raw land is minimal. The biggest increase in land values is at the very beginning, when raw land is moving from real raw land into acreage plots. When land moves from acreage plots into lots, there's less increase in price and less profit. When it moves from lots into building sites, there's even less. Therefore, the time to get raw land for the biggest profit is early in the game. That is not always easy to do.

145

Location

Where should you buy raw land? What are some of the things to look for in order to get the advantage of the big increase at the beginning of the development of an area? Appraisers have a general rule they use about the value of land in terms of an investment. They say there are three things you should look for in buying land: location, jobs, and climate. There are other factors, but let's consider these first. The most important one of all is location. You may find the most beautiful land as far as topography, view, fertility of the soil, and price are concerned, but you need a location where value will count and increase your initial investment.

Jobs

What are the things that make a location a good location? Up at the top of the list is *jobs!* There are exceptions, such as in the case of attractive recreational property—for example, a sea coast; a lake front; or perhaps a desert area or a spa. This kind of property, however, is usually unstable in value. When times get tough, people find they can get along quite well without going to vacation spots. They'll struggle through the year without it somehow.

The most important thing is jobs. Further, these should be jobs that are going to be there a while. They should be stable jobs in stable industries—jobs that are not susceptible to being shifted. People move where the jobs are, even if the location is not pleasant. They go where they can earn a living.

Analyze the economic basis of the area. Drive around the area and look at the buildings. Find out who owns them and who leases. If they are owned by big corporations, you can often feel more secure about the economic future of the area. A word of caution: what seems to be big capital investment of an industry in a particular area may not, indeed, be a capital investment of that industry. The industry may only be leasing space. The kind of industry it is will give you a better clue. If it is a highly volatile type that depends on defense contracts, for example, it may not be stable enough for your investment. If the contracts are cancelled, as they often are, the economy of the area could be hurt. Land values will also be hurt.

Climate

Climate is the next important consideration after jobs. Climate is important because it can make your job miserable if, for example, the weather is too hot and humid for you. If you could have the same kind of job for about the same pay, the chances are you would favor a warm climate to a cold, wet one.

Public Services

Public service aspects of the location would include: the kind of government facilities provided for the people living in the district and the availability of such things as fire protection, police protection, schools, sidewalks, curbs, streets, and so on. Obviously, you're not going to find such things as sidewalks, curbs, and streetlights, yet you will ultimately have to get these to obtain top profits on raw land. Some developers buy the land and get it annexed by a city. If a city annexes raw land, it may provide these things. If the land can't be developed easily, then potential buyers aren't going to buy it. People aren't going to want to live there.

Leisure Opportunities

The availability of leisure facilities such as recreational facilities and cultural facilities is also important. The raw land may be fairly far out, but a freeway could bring motion picture theatres, music centers, and recreational activities closer. In some cases, the raw land might even be adjacent to a leisure area. People are getting more and more leisure time. More and more they prefer to live where there are leisure facilities.

Higher Education

One important factor for plants that employ a large number of well-educated personnel is nearby colleges or universities, that offer degrees beyond the Bachelor's degree. This is because a good many of their people are interested in pursuing advanced degrees. One of the things that will attract an engineer, a chemist, or a geologist to live and work there is if he can pursue his work on his Masters or his PhD. The opportunity for self-improvement is an important factor. No one of the factors mentioned, other than jobs, is absolutely vital. It's the combination of these things. The ideal location would have all of these.

Timing

Timing is important. The day that somebody announces they are going to build a plant employing 5,000 or 6,000 people out in the middle of nowhere, is one day too late for the investor who wants top profits. The raw land price goes up immediately. Buy the property the day before they announce it and sell it the day after.

Analysis of Trends

There are a lot of factors involved in profitable land speculation. Banks, trade and civic organizations, colleges and universities, the state, and the federal government all generate a tremendous amount of statistics and economic data to help guide you in analyzing all the factors that affect land values. Let's just take one example. As mentioned, jobs are a key factor to land value. You should always be alert, therefore, to leads concerning new job possibilities. For example, a significant development may be reported in the newspaper. Many people will read about it and not grasp immediately the full significance. Suppose it is a bond issue that has been passed to build a giant irrigation project. The average person who reads that will think, "Fine, we're going to have water." However, the sophisticated investor will think, "What does this mean in terms of permanent jobs and where?"

New Developments = New Jobs

You may read that there's going to be a plant at this location, or you may discover where there's to be a large pumping station, transfer station, or distribution point. You may find that a permanent staff of 2,000 to 5,000 people will be hired. All this means jobs, and jobs mean increased land values.

Take another example, Eastern manufacturers of a variety of consumer goods ship things to the Pacific Coast market. This will keep up until they notice the market for their product on the Pacific Coast is getting so large that much of their profit is being eaten up in freight costs. They decide that it would be cheaper to manufacture or assemble the product on the Pacific Coast. To illustrate: Some years ago the Chevrolet people realized that California was one of their biggest markets. So instead of assembling cars in Detroit and shipping them across country, they now assemble them in California. The wise investor watches for information of such plant locations and tries to get raw land nearby.

Another illustration: The Dow-Jones Company found out that about 70% of their total subscriptions of the Pacific Coast edition of the *Wall Street Journal* were from Los Angeles. Yet, the *Wall Street Journal* plant was in San Francisco. It didn't take long for management to decide that it was smarter to build or lease a plant in Los Angeles. The same thing is true of the food industry. Food producers tend to follow national population immigrations so as to be close to their customers. Here again, the wise investor watches, weighs, and invests ahead of the crowd.

Where Will People and Industry Seek Land?

Where will they all move? Where would Dow-Jones put a plant to publish the *Wall Street Journal?* Just analyze its needs and you can almost predict where they will locate. First of all, it's a newspaper that requires daily distribution. Since 70% is going to be distributed in Los Angeles, this means street transportation is of prime importance. The plant should be located at a place where there is good transportation. Since 30% of the newspapers have to be shipped out of the area by plane, it should be close to an airport. They want to buy the cheapest possible land they can get. They need a good location with room for expansion. Look for locations that satisfy these needs and you have a good idea of where Dow-Jones will locate. In other words, you go through the same search and elimination process as the scout looking for the plant location.

Physical Factors

The physical aspects of the property are important if you are going to buy right. The usefulness of the property is the key consideration. Size, shape, area, soil, and topography are all factors that decide how useable the property will be. The easier it is to develop, the greater its value.

Financial Factors

The financial situation is important, now and later, in terms of the kind of property you are going to buy. Is it industrial, residential, or commercial property? What kind of a money market is there now? What kind of a money market has there been traditionally in the past? What is reasonable to expect in the future in terms of financing available to develop this kind of property? You may think that is the next buyer's problem, but it isn't. If a person can't get the money to develop, he isn't going to buy. So you care very much about his problems. Go talk to some bankers. Talk to people who are in the business and find out about what the market is on office buildings, shopping centers, and so on.

Social Factors

There are social problems that might create difficulties for the land investment you make. Not the least of these is integration and racial tensions. It's a very real problem. It doesn't matter what your feeling is about it. The point is we are living in a transition time. When the transition is over, and nobody cares about the skin color of the man that lives next door, then there will be no problems. But before that time arrives, there are problems. The man who is going to buy the raw land from you and develop it is going to care about these problems because they affect his ability to rent space. In fact, there are some developers who have gotten out of the residential housing market (no more apartment buildings, no more single-family tracts; at least not until things simmer down). They are constructing commercial buildings or something else.

Government Regulations

What kind of government regulations apply to land and its development? The building codes and zoning regulations exist in most areas. They limit what you can do with the land. You should determine if there is a master plan of the area and how it affects the property you're considering buying. The land you're buying probably isn't in the city yet. It's probably in the country. Nevertheless, what kind of restrictions are they going to put on this property?

In other words, you may think that you're going to be able to sell the property to somebody who can build five houses to an acre on it. Then you look at the master plan, and you talk to some of their planners. You find out they won't allow more than two houses per acre on that land. This seriously affects the price you can get for it.

What to Pay

What should you pay for raw land? Assume that you have raw acreage. You plan on selling it to a man who is going to subdivide it into lots. He is not going to build on it. He's just going to sell the lots. The first thing you want to figure out is what will *he* be able to sell these lots for after he develops them? You may have to look ahead a bit and do some estimating.

Also, how many lots can he get per acre? That's where the government regulations come in. That's where the physical lay-of-the-land comes in, too. If it's rolling or hilly, you are not going to get as many lots or houses per acre as if it is level. If the building and zoning regulations require so many square feet of land per lot, that's going to limit how many he can get out of an acre. The average city lot usually runs about 5,000 square feet in size. As a rule-of-thumb, he will normally get about five or six lots per acre after all streets and public improvements are taken into account.

An Example

Let's assume he can get five lots per acre that you estimate can be sold for $5,000 per lot or $25,000 per acre. From this estimated income figure, you must subtract four categories of deductions:

1. *The Cost to Create the Lots.* What will it cost to put in the sidewalks, the curbs, the streetlights, the sewers, and all the things required to produce a finished lot? Let's say it costs $1,500 per lot. So, for five lots it is going to cost him $7,500.

2. *The Cost to Carry This Property.* These are expenses he will have after he buys the raw land from you and before he sells the finished lots. This will include such things as real estate taxes and interest on his investment. These are fairly easy to calculate with some certainty. Let's say it costs him $4,000 per acre to carry it.

3. *The Cost to Market the Lots.* He can hire a real estate broker and pay him a commission, or he can put up his own little office and have a telephone, a secretary, or salesman. This would be expensive. If he hires a broker, he will pay him whatever is the standard commission on vacant land. Let's say it's 10% commission. Thus, on the sale of $25,000, he is going to pay $2,500 commission per acre.

4. *The Kind of Profit He Desires.* Lets say he wants a 20% profit. So the 20% of the income must go to profit. This would be $5,000.

Add these up quickly and you get $19,000. This is what it's going to "cost" the man who buys the raw land from you. It's going to "cost" him $19,000 to come out on this deal. The maximum that he can pay you for your raw land is $6,000 an acre. If he pays more to you, there is only one place he can get the money and that's by cutting his profit. That is not too popular with developers.

POINTS TO KEEP IN MIND

Factors that affect land value are:

- *Location.*
- *Jobs.*
- *Climate.*
- *Public services.*
- *Leisure opportunities.*
- *Higher education.*
- *Timing.*
- *Trends.*

Some of the factors that determine plant locations and, in turn, bring jobs are:

- *Physical factors.*
- *Financial factors.*
- *Social factors.*
- *Government regulations.*

What should you pay for raw land? Here's one good approach:

- *Estimate fair market value of improved land ready to develop.*
- *Subtract cost of creating improvements.*
- *Subtract cost of carrying property.*
- *Subtract cost of selling property.*
- *Subtract allowance for profit.*
- *The result equals what you can afford to pay for raw land.*

···14···

Investing in
Apartment Houses

Apartment houses are an interesting subject in many ways. There is a big supply of them, and they are a major form of investment property. Many times the question is asked whether an apartment house is a good investment. Without trying to evade the question, I would have to say it depends on what your investment objective is. Over a period of ten or 15 years, a carefully purchased apartment building can be a very good investment. However, you must recognize what you are getting into, in terms of your investment.

Traditional Apartment Dwellers

First of all, the groups of people in our population that are traditionally

153

apartment dwellers, are growing more rapidly than the groups of people that are traditionally homeowners or home occupiers. Young married couples, before they have children, are traditionally apartment dwellers. The older people, whose children have grown up and moved out of the house, become apartment dwellers. The single-person household, the widower, the widow, the unmarried single person, the bachelor, and the unmarried girl may be apartment dwellers.

Apartment Housing Demand

There are more people demanding housing, and we are running out of land. This results in a stronger and stronger tendency toward more intensive use of the land. Now, let me illustrate what I mean. After World War II, there was a so-called, "flight to the suburbs." Everybody rushed out to buy a home with the help of the GI, the FHA, and State Veteran loans. The reason they chose the suburbs was because the builder could build a better home there. Because his land cost was lower, he could afford to put more dollars into the building. Wives were particularly impressed with the designs, and they had a lot to do with the decision on the home. People went to the suburbs and they thought this was one of the truly great American dreams. They could own their own home.

Just go out into a tract in the suburbs on any given Saturday or Sunday and you'll find that everybody's out in front weeding or putting in a new lawn. The Great Dream didn't turn out to be exactly what they had envisioned. Those people found out they could buy the house for $500 down, but in the first year they put another $1,000 in a fence, etc. A lot of people found that what they saved by going farther out was really being spent in gasoline, oil, and tires. Their total living expenses did not decrease. If anything, they increased. The total aggravation rate of husbands increased significantly.

In the mid-fifties, we began to see a movement back toward the city. The movement has not stopped going to the suburbs, but it's not going out as far, and it's not going out as strongly as it used to. More people want to move closer in. So, there's a great demand for land closer to urban centers.

The Ford Foundation made an economic analysis of the needs of the United States in the year 2000. The study revealed that one of the great economic shortages this country will face is of land. It is estimated that if you threw in every bit of land that we have in the United States—

including deserts, swamps, and mountains—we would still be short 50 million acres of land. In California they are urbanizing land at the rate of 300 acres per day. That doesn't sound like much, but 300 acres a day times 365 days of the year is a lot.

Apartments Are Work

So land has to be used more intensively. Thus, in the long run, apartments will have a good future. However, bear in mind that when you buy an apartment house, you're also buying a lot of work. The work that has to be done, maybe not by you, but, if not by you, than by someone you hire to do it.

This includes collecting the rents, paying the bills, taking care of the yards, and renting the property when it's vacant. Operating an apartment house is a business, and you should recognize it as such. You can't look at the apartment and say, "I'm going to invest $10,000 in an apartment building, and I'm going to get $2,000 net return on this investment." You are not going to get $2,000 return on your investment. You are going to get $2,000 return on your investment *and* your part-time job. Perhaps after you subtract what your part-time job should be paying, you will be getting about a $1,000 return. I'm not saying that 10% return on your investment is bad. What I am saying is that you should recognize the situation for what it actually is.

The Neighborhood

If you are going to buy an apartment building, find an area that appears to be a good apartment house neighborhood. Go through it. See what is available. A good apartment house neighborhood is one that has things which are attractive to the *tenants*. The tenant is the one who is going to pay the bills.

Employment

So you want to pick a location that is attractive to tenants. What kind of a location is that? One of the big elements is employment. The location should be fairly convenient to employment. The more employment that it is convenient to, the better. Ideally, it should not be next to employment. That's a little too close. But generally, it should be within 20 minutes' to a half hour's travel time.

Recreation

It should be convenient to shopping and to leisure-time activity. The *kind* of leisure-time activities will depend on the kind of tenants to whom you wish to appeal. If you want to attract younger families with a few children, or those with no children, or unmarrieds, then you probably want your apartment building close to such things as theatres and night-life activities. If you are appealing to families with children, then you want it convenient to schools. The type of schools will depend on the ages of the children involved. You would be interested in playgrounds and libraries, rather than parks and senior citizen clubhouses. If you are going to appeal to an older segment of the population, you're interested in the kind of leisure-time activities that will appeal to more mature people.

Transportation

You should be concerned with transportation. The kind of transportation depends again on the type of tenant to whom you are renting. If you are renting to a low-income tenant, you need to be convenient to public transportation. If you are appealing to middle-upper income tenants, then you need to be convenient to a good traffic grid, close to freeways and main arteries.

Go through the neighborhood and see what kind of tenants now live there. That will give you a clue as to the kind of tenants to which you should be appealing. You can see how many children there are around. You can get an idea of the economic class of the tenants from the kinds of automobiles you see parked in the garages. Of course, that can be deceiving. For example, the Volkswagen has become a status symbol for people with Rolls Royces and Cadillacs. But obviously there's a Ford, Chevy, Plymouth category and there's a Pontiac, Oldsmobile, Buick category. That's not a sure test, but it gives you an idea. You care about that, because you want to know how much rent you can really expect to collect in this neighborhood.

Neighborhood Life Cycles

Classically, neighborhoods go through a three-phase cycle: development, stability, and decline. If there are many lots in the neighborhood that haven't been built upon, it may very well be still in the development phase. This is a good time to get in. On the other hand, if you find that it is a neighborhood where most of the buildings are older and where single-family homes in the neighborhood are tenant occupied, the neighborhood might be on the decline. The area will probably look rundown. This is not necessarily bad, provided that you know what you're getting into.

Comparison Shopping

The next thing you might do is go around the neighborhood alone and act as if you wanted to rent an apartment. When you come out of the apartment, make some notes about what it offers. How big is the apartment? Is it well lighted and airy? Does it have all the "gingerbread" that appeals to tenants, such as the built-in oven and stove and air conditioner? Does it have the drapes and carpets? What kind of concessions are suggested to you by the manager when you don't show great enthusiasm for signing a lease immediately? Does he offer you a couple of months' rent free? What kind of a deal is he going to make? Now you can get kind of an idea what the going rent is in this neighborhood. Then look at an apartment in the building you are thinking of buying. Compare apartments in that building with what you've found to be the average apartment in the neighborhood. What is the average monthly rent? You compare that rent with that of the apartments in the building you are looking at. Are the apartments in this building better or worse? This is your merchandise on the shelf which you are going to have to rent to some other person. Which apartment would you rather rent?

Property Income

Now figure out how much income this building will bring. Suppose you have ten apartments at $100 a month. This comes to $12,000 a year. Allow for vacancies. The *scheduled* rent is what the owner thinks it ought to rent for *if* it was rented. Curiously, if all the other apartments in this neighborhood are renting for $95 a month, he may schedule his vacant apartments at $125. The owner figures that makes it look better. You are interested in facts, so forget about the scheduled rent. Instead, make your own estimation of what this apartment ought to be renting for to be in competition with all the other apartments in the neighborhood. How many vacancies are in the neighborhood? What is your competition? It's not bad to have vacancies in an apartment building, as long as you recognize them and take them into account. You could buy a building and afford to have 50% vacancies, provided that you bought the right one. This, of course, is an exaggeration. You should also consider the *trend* of rents in the area. You may be getting $100 a month now, but what about next year and the year after that? You should adjust your gross income calculations accordingly.

Operating Statements

Look over the operating statements very carefully. You may find that the ones the previous owner kept are not complete. If the building has any maturity at all, he should be able to show you operating statements for the last two to five years.

1. *Operating Expenses.*

Operating expenses will vary directly in proportion to the number of tenants you have. When the apartment building is completely filled, your operating expenses will be the highest. When you have the building completely vacant, the expenses will be the lowest. Operating expenses include such things as rubbish collection, yard maintenance, and utilities. There are some utilities that the owner pays for and some that the tenant absorbs.

There is also the cost of management. Figure that in, too. What are you going to have to pay for management? The best arrangement for management depends on the property. In many states, you must have a resident manager on the premises when the building exceeds a certain number of apartments.

a. *Resident Managers*

It is often best to find a couple who are steady people and don't drink. This is an important factor. Check on the drinking. If you find somebody who has a good trade, is steady, and has a history of employment, this could be your answer. These people might normally be able to rent a $75 or $80 apartment; you move them into an apartment that would rent for $100. You will find that these people are the best kind of managers. They have a regard for the kind of place that they are now living in. This works out especially well if the man is handy and can take care of odds and ends around the apartment building. You might want to pay him a little extra for repainting apartments or doing certain work. The wife can take care of collecting rent and miscellaneous things of that sort.

b. *Paying Managers*

You will have to decide what to pay your managers. One way is to calculate it on an hourly basis. Figure about how much work they have to do in terms of hours. How many hours does the wife spend collecting rent and paying bills? How much time does the husband spend on taking care of the yard, and other miscellaneous things? If they are going to spend 30 hours a month between them, you will have a pretty good idea of about what you should pay them. You might allow a figure generally between $1.60 and $2.50 an hour. This will vary with local pay scales. I have found that it is always better to pay a little bit more. I'd rather pay somebody $2.50 or more an hour if they are good. The difference is really negligible for what you get. They should do little extra things which make your tenants happier and which make them think they are in a well-managed building.

Technically, you are required to file a social security report. You must pay social security taxes and deduct it from their wages (even if you aren't paying in cash but in reduced rent). Whether you do or not is between you and your conscience. Many people do not. I understand that the government may start clamping down on the bigger units where such deductions are not now made.

c. *Maintenance Instructions*

Be sure to instruct your managers on how to take care of minor repairs, such as how to unstick the garbage disposal. They should know where the power and gas cutoffs are for each apartment, and how to turn them off. They should know where the master water valve is. You should be sure the warranty tags for the hot water heaters have been sent in to the manufacturer. It's also a good idea to check and flush hot water heaters out every six months. Incidentally, often the warranty doesn't apply unless a master plumber installs it.

The resident manager should help you with preventative maintenance by making periodic inspections. For example, before the rainy season, someone should go up on the roof with a hose and wet it down. This is one way to see if there are any leaks in the upper apartments. The hardest time to get a roofer is when it is raining. This should be done in the late summertime, before the rainy season starts. The manager should go around and check the outside lights frequently. He should have a petty cash fund, so he can have a supply of electric light bulbs for all the public areas. This will reduce your liability exposure. Have them look for cracks in the sidewalk, in the balconies, in the driveway, or wherever a woman might catch her heel or injure herself. Make sure that there is nothing such as a rosebush or a hedge sticking out so someone could hurt himself. On wood or plastered building corners exposed to car traffic, you might want to put up some kind of bumper guard to save you expensive repair jobs.

d. *Tenants and Maintenance*

Have the manager instruct new tenants on how to take care of little things for themselves. He should instruct the tenants on what to do when there is a plumbing stoppage. He should explain where the cutoff valve is for the water and gas. The tenant should be informed that there are certain things you do not put down garbage disposals, such as celery, artichoke leaves, and corn husks. If the garbage disposal gets stuck, they should know how to unstick it.

Every meter in the building should be labelled, as well as the master cutoff valve for the water and electricity in each apartment. All these little things will save you a tremendous amount of money and maintenance, particularly if you've got a man who looks out for these things. Have this man carefully inspect the building outside and inside, and the public areas, at least once every three months.

2. *Repair and Maintenance Expenses.*

You also have what is called repair and maintenance expenses, which include such things as replacing hot water heaters when they go out, fixing garbage disposals, repairing leaky roofs, and redecorating. If a tenant has lived there a year or two, he will stay another year only if you repaint for him. That's often a lot cheaper than if you let him move out.

3. *Fixed Expenses.*

Fixed expenses are things that don't vary with the number of tenants you have. They are not *absolutely* fixed, but they change little from year to year. This includes insurance and real estate taxes.

Financial Analysis

Deduct all these expenses from gross income. This will give you the net income before you've made any mortgage payments and before you've taken off for any depreciation. You can work these figures around toward any objective you want—taxable income, return on investment, etc. You should first find out what the total return on the property is before you have to borrow money to buy it and before you take up tax shelter. If the total price of the building is such that you make 6% on the total price and it costs 8% to borrow money, it's not a good deal.

It is this kind of analysis you must make to determine what you should pay for a property. Many foolish investors look only at the return on their down payment. They ignore the fact that the portion of the total return the down payment gets is the first thing to get cut when there are vacancies or other problems. Take that into consideration when you think just in terms of the return on your down payment.

The Trust Deed Pitfall

There are a couple of other little tricks you should watch for when you consider buying an apartment house. Say it's for sale at a certain price, perhaps $100,000. And, suppose there is a spread of $40,000 between the existing financing and the price. This is more than you want to pay or can pay down, so the seller suggests you get a new loan. The new first loan is $75,000; the owner will take back a $10,000 second trust deed; and, the broker will take his commission of $6,000 in a third trust deed. So you, as the new owner, are taking a property with a first, second, and third trust deed. It might work out, but bear in mind that you will have to service all these debts or face losing the original investment.

A Rule-of-Thumb

As a quick rule-of-thumb, your total expenses should run on the average between 30 and 40% of actual income. Mortgages should be able to be serviced by not more than 50% of the income of the property. In other words, if you're faced with a situation where it takes, for example, 65 or 70% of the total income when the building is 100% occupied just to meet the mortgage payment, you stand a good chance of losing your investment.

How Heavy a Debt Load?

How heavy a debt load can the property carry? This depends on what the payments are, and this is a function of two things: interest and the length of time in which you have to pay the loan off. If you've got $91,000 against this building in three trust deeds, all at 30 years and 5½% interest, you may be safe. On the other hand, if the first is a 15-year mortgage at 8.5%; and the second and third are for three years at 10%, you may have trouble making the payments because there are several expenses that you cannot put off. You can stall on some of your maintenance and management, but you can't delay your tax collector, insurance, or utilities. There are certain things that have to be paid. So you have mandatory operating and fixed expenses plus the income needed to pay the notes and trust deeds.

Other Pitfalls

There are several hazards to watch for when you buy the building. Seek homogeneous tenants. They will stay longer, especially if they're older people. Notice also what types of wall surfaces the building has. Brick walls have to be redone occasionally but are low maintenance. Stucco finishes need more repainting attention and wood usually needs the most care. Consider these extra expenses when you make your investment decision.

Watch Secondary Financing Terms

Most real estate purchases require some kind of financing beyond the first mortgage or first trust deed. Often the seller will carry back a secondary note to complete the needed financing. Sometimes the terms of this secondary financing can put you in such a box that you have no room to move around in reselling or refinancing the property to your best advantage.

Some of the things to watch from a business viewpoint include:

1. *Acceleration Clause*—This is a provision that makes the note due and payable in full in the event that you sell the property to a subsequent buyer. When you are the first buyer, avoid letting the seller put such a clause in any secondary note.

2. *Succession to Primary Position*—Some secondary notes are made to be inferior in claims against the property only up to the first mortgage or first trust deed of record at the time of the sale. In other words, if you were to pay off the original first mortgage or first trust deed, the secondary note would automatically move into first priority. This would virtually preclude any further bank or institutional financing until this note was paid off, too. Secondary notes should be specified as inferior to all first mortgages and first trust deeds made now or in the future against the property.

3. *Prepayment of Secondary Notes*—Sometimes you will find it to your advantage to be able to pay off the secondary note in advance of its due date. For this reason, it is important to specify the periodic payments as so much, "or more," per installment. If you don't put the *or more* in your contract, you cannot double up in payments when times are good with-

out paying a penalty. In other words, you can't pay the note off in advance. The person who holds the second trust deed often wants only that interest, while hoping you will get in a jam some time and default. This would allow him to foreclose the property which may be very profitable for him.

Buy Big

Always buy the biggest place you can. There are more economies you can get out of a larger place than you can from a smaller. As a matter of fact, an apartment building isn't really regarded as investment property unless it has 16 or 18 units. An example of the economies of large building size is the swimming pool. In many types of apartments, you need to have a swimming pool to attract tenants. If you have a ten-unit building, and it costs you $50 a month for chemicals and service to keep that pool in operation, you've got to get $5 more rent per apartment just to cover the cost of the pool. But for the same size pool you might be able to service 30 units. In this case, you only need $1.67 more a month per apartment to cover the pool cost.

Another concern with apartments is the problem of a better product coming on the market. In the period right after World War II, the usual apartment building was a frame and stucco two-story walkup. They had double-hung wooden windows, no air conditioning, and no carpeting. They could be built for about $6.50 a square foot. Within five years they were faced with competition from buildings containing aluminum sash windows, air conditioning, built-in oven-stoves, sauna baths, swimming pools, and a game room. You have to update the building to compete or lower the rent.

If you want to rent, a good idea is to contact large organizations within the general limits of your renting area, such as colleges and large employers. They often maintain files of potential tenants. Most of these will set down certain minimal requirements that you must meet. All in all, apartment buildings are a lot of work but can be a good investment, because the demand for them is increasing as cities become more and more urbanized and prime city land becomes increasingly scarce.

POINTS TO KEEP IN MIND

- *Apartment houses have a good future in this country.*
- *Apartment properties are work, and to be a success they must be oriented to what tenants want and need. They must provide:*

—*Proximity to jobs.*
—*Convenient recreation, shopping, and transportation.*
—*Neighborhood and co-tenants who are compatible.*

- *In analyzing an apartment property, check the neighborhood; do comparison shopping; carefully analyze the income statements (also called "operating statements"); and, avoid getting into a property that is a burden on your financial resources.*
- *However, try to buy as big as you can. This is not contradictory to my previous admonition. Don't overburden your financial resources but don't go so small that there is no real profit, either.*

···15···

Retail Stores
as an Investment

===

Many investors find retail store property, either as a single retail store or in some kind of shopping center, an exceptionally good investment. So, this chapter will dwell on this a bit. The lease checklist (covered in Chapter 20) is an important adjunct to this chapter, in terms of the soundness of the investment.

Tenants—Your Unofficial Partners

The reason for this is that so much of the value in retail stores depends upon the success of the tenant occupying the store. The landlord's share of that success is a function of the kind of lease he has. The reason I say the landlord's share of that success is fairly simple, is because every landlord of a retail tenant is also a partner of that retail tenant—whether the landlord wants to be or not. In other words, unless the tenant makes a success of the store, the landlord will not make a success of renting that store to him. Unfortunately, too many landlords look upon retail tenants as just somebody to pay the rent, and the way in which the tenant raises the money to pay that rent is ignored by the landlord. This is a very serious mistake! Because, as I have said before, a lease is only as good as the man who signs it. And, if it is difficult or impossible for the man to make a living in a retail store location, he is going to find the rent payment unbearable. On the other hand, the man who is making a success of his retail store operation regards the rent as one of the least expensive of his overhead items.

Generally speaking, I'll be talking about retail stores in the traditional sense as opposed to some of the different variations that have come into being over recent years. An enclosed store, usually on the ground floor, in which there is a merchant selling goods or services at retail, will be the type of store referred to. It may be an individual store out on the highway which is what some particular merchants prefer, or it may be in a boulevard-type business development that is so common along the main streets of many American communities. Also, it may be a store in a shopping center—one of many varying sizes.

Investment Factors

There are a number of important factors that go into making a retail store location successful, and these same factors affect the soundness of this store as an investment from the point of view of the investor. As just mentioned, the factors that make for a successful retail merchant also make for a successful retail merchant's landlord. For various kinds of retail operations, there are special factors that enter into the site selection. These can't be dealt with here because of the vast number of variations for different retail operations.

However, I can enumerate some of the generally important things and leave it to you to investigate some of the specific factors in connection with a particular site you may be considering.

1. *Location.*

There is an old rule in the retail business that the three most important factors to consider are location, location, and location. Among the smart, successful merchants, there is a dedication to getting a good location for their business—in fact, the *best* location—because in a

bad location, you can't do the business. The bad location is probably
the most expensive one, because it costs just as much money to construct the building and put in the fixtures in a bad location as it does
in a good location. The main difference is in the value of the land. The
merchant in a bad location will find that rent is a higher percentage
of his overhead expenses than it is in a good one because he is not
doing the volume of business. And, the landlord, the fixture people,
and all the money that has been invested in the building—these have
to get the same kind of return as in the marketplace. Therefore, the
only variation is the kind of return you're going to get on the difference
in land value. Good merchants realize this but poor merchants don't.
These are always choosing the weaker locations and, as a result, they
are continually doing poorer business than their cousins in the better
locations. So, from the point of view of the investor, it's better to get
an excellent location than it is to get the secondary location, because
you'll attract a smarter tenant—one who is more likely to be successful
and who will be more stable as a tenant for you. Whether you invest
in a good location or a bad location, you are going to get the same
kind of return from a percentage point of view when you consider
the stability of the tenant.

2. *Accessibility.*

The ease with which the potential customer can get to your merchant-
tenant is very important to that tenant's success. Unfortunately, too
many investors do not recognize this and too many merchants don't
either. It's one thing for a tenant to have the best merchandise, provide good service, and all the other things that a good operator will
provide—but, if nobody can get to him, he's not going to do any
business. When I'm talking about accessibility, I'm talking about it
from several points of view. Today, this country is largely automobile
oriented; therefore, the accessibility of the merchant's store by automobile is important. There are still some areas where it's easy to shop
by public transportation. The shortcoming of this, however, is that
all of those people who shop using public transportation have to carry
their bundles to and from the bus, or the subway, or whatever public
transportation they are using. This limits the number of purchases
they make because it just becomes physically too difficult to purchase
more than they can handle—unless it's merchandise that is going to be
delivered, of course. With a car, however, people can shop and buy
a lot more because they can put it in baskets, trundle it out to the car,
and drive it home. So, accessibility by car is very important.

The rise of the shopping center at the edge of the old, traditional
commercial districts while those very districts were falling on very
lean years is proof of what I'm saying here. Most of those old commercial districts did not provide easy accessibility for a car. They

didn't provide parking. They didn't provide wide enough streets. In fact, they did many things that tended to aggravate drivers; such as, allowing through traffic to mix with local traffic, putting parking meters on the streets, and creating other obstacles. Because of their failure to accommodate the automobile, they have suffered a decline from which they have, mostly, not recovered. Those few old-time traditional shopping districts which have recovered from these declines have been those that have instituted the changes necessary to make them more attractive for the car.

There are a lot of people who criticize the nation's car-centered culture and, while what they say may be true or not, the fact does remain, from the point of view of the investor, that you've got to have easy accessibility from a car. This means that you want to avoid locations where there are, as I implied before, high-speed through traffic mixed with local traffic; where there is a divider in the highway so that people cannot turn left to get across to the store's location; and where there is not enough effective parking and other aspects of accessibility.

3. *Effective Parking*.

A word about effective parking. By effective parking, I mean parking spaces that are actually used by most of the customers. This is as contrasted to the total number of parking spaces. Many parking spaces are really either inadequate or almost a waste of space because they are hardly even used. There is an effective parking zone that extends as a band around most stores for a distance of somewhere between 150 and 250 feet, because people do not want to park their cars and walk farther than that. If you want proof of this, just visit a shopping center on any busy weekend and you will see that all of the parking spaces within a radius of 150 to 250 feet from the stores will be filled constantly. And, even if there are a lot of parking spaces beyond that distance, you will see cars circling around and around, ignoring those spaces and looking for spaces within the effective parking zone.

4. *Parking Stall Design*.

In addition, effective parking refers to parking spaces that people can and will park in. Unfortunately, there are some architects and builders who mislead department stores and their clients by designing parking lots which have spaces laid out in such a way that they are too small and cramped. Customers very quickly get aggravated trying to park in these narrow spaces and shy away from doing business with the merchants who are served by this type of parking area.

For example, about the actual minimum size you can make a parking stall is something on the order of 18 feet long by 8 feet wide. This is so minimal that people just aren't going to use it if they can avoid it. They will go someplace else where they can park more comfortably. A good-sized parking space should be 20 feet long and 9 feet wide with double lines between each stall, to allow people room to get in and out of their cars with the packages you hope they are going to be buying from the merchants who are your tenants. Also, the angle of the parking is important. Sometimes an attempt is made to squeeze as many parking spaces onto a lot as possible. This can be done by putting the stalls at right angles to the aisle. However, this makes it very difficult for anybody to pull in and out of the stalls—particularly women. So, I urge that parking and other accessibility factors be carefully investigated before you make any kind of investment.

5. *Area Buying Power.*

Buying power is one of the most important things to consider. If you put a department store in the middle of a coral atoll, 1,000 miles out in the Pacific Ocean, it wouldn't take much to predict that the department store is going to fail because there are no customers. Yet, a lot of investors do the same thing with stores, in essence, by putting them down in the middle of what really amounts to a desert of buying power—where there is just no buying power for the particular product they've got. This is even more inexcusable when you realize how much statistical material is available to help you determine what the buying power of an area is. The Census Bureau, the Department of Commerce, as well as local Chambers of Commerce, planning departments, schools and universities, banks, financial institutions, real estate boards, etc., put out so much material about most of the urban communities in America that your problem is one of picking and choosing. The real problem is one of how to avoid being drowned in all this material.

There are many statistical tables published which are helpful in determining any buying power. For example, you may run across a table that illustrates the number of families and the typical annual sales volume that are needed to support various kinds of stores. Let's take a bookstore. Our table says that it takes approximately 12,800 families to support a bookstore. Obviously, if you're going into a community where there are only 5,000 families, you are going to have a difficult time supporting a bookstore. You can't expect a bookstore in that location to succeed. So, if you buy a property rented to a bookstore on a long lease, or if you lease a vacant store you have to a bookstore in that kind of situation, you are just asking for trouble. You also have to consider what the competition is, because if you have a community of 25,000 families, this should be enough to support two bookstores. But, what if there are already two bookstores? Then, of course, you wouldn't want to add a third.

6. *Location Drawing Power.*

It is absolutely critical for a great many tenants to have certain other types of businesses near them that draw customers to the location. For this reason, major shopping centers will frequently lease space to a giant department store, variety, or drugstore for relatively low rent in order to get the drawing power of these major advertisers, who are aggressive, smart operators. Then, they turn around and jack up the rent commensurately higher for the smaller tenants who benefit by the association with this major drawing tenant to offset rental losses incurred. It would not be unusual, for example, at current prices, to rent to a major tenant in many locations for $1.25 to $1.50 per square foot per year. In the same area adjacent to the major tenant, you might be renting to a smaller tenant for anywhere from $4 to $12 per square foot per year. So the smaller tenant pays for the drawing power of the big one, but this is the way it works and it works out to everyone's satisfaction. This is so important that some small tenants insist on co-tenancy clauses which allow them to cancel their leases if the major tenant ceases doing business there.

7. *Competition.*

As mentioned earlier, there is a question of competition. The competition for the merchants that are your tenants is also competition for you as a landlord because it affects the success of the tenant with whom you are indirectly in partnership. How good is the competition? How close is it? How strong is it? Is it aggressive and well run? Does it have a stronger drawing power than your people have? Has it got better accessibility? What about the purchasing power? How much of the buying power in the community will this other tenant draw? This is very important to weigh against who you are going to lease to or what kind of store you are going to buy as an investor, in terms of the tenant that is guaranteeing the lease. To use the example cited before, with two bookstores in a town of 25,000 families, if you need 12,800 families per bookstore—then, obviously, there is no room for a third as far as competition is concerned.

8. *Public Services.*

What about public services? How available are they to the property in question? Is there good fire and police protection? Police protection is extremely important in this era of very high burglary rates in most parts of the country. What about fire protection? What about public utilities in the form of gas, electricity, water, and sewers? All of these are very important. Without the necessary public utilities and services, the costs of construction and maintenance rise very markedly. And, they can hurt your profits and ability to service the property and keep the tenant.

9. *Lease Terms.*

Then, what about lease terms? I've discussed these at some length in Chapter 20. You should review them very carefully if you are going to invest in a property, because lease terms are critical in determining the amount, the stability, and the length of the income streams that are absolutely vital for the support of a good return on your investment.

10. *Trends in the Community.*

What about the trends in the area where you're contemplating buying a store or contemplating buying any kind of retail property? You, after all, are going to have to live with the decision for some time. Which way is the trend going in this neighborhood? Is it going up or is it stabilized? Is it going down? What is the trend of the buying power? Have the kind of people that are living here changed substantially from those who were living here? Is the neighborhood getting people with greater buying power or lower buying power? What about the trend of competition? Is more competition coming into the area? What is the profile of the population in this area? This is to say, how many people are there in a family? If you have large families, then you're talking about stores that cater to family selling—which means medium- and low-priced clothing, shoe stores, variety stores, and department stores that are in the low- to medium-price ranges, such as a Sears, Roebuck or a Wards. You're not looking toward a high-class department store like Sak's Fifth Avenue or I. Magnin, or something of that sort.

11. *Physical Property.*

The physical property that you are contemplating—is it a good size that can accommodate a number of different types of stores so that you have the drawing power and all these other advantages, but without being so big that it is difficult to get around without getting back in the car? If someone has to move his car once he's in the shopping center to get to another end of it, you could be in trouble as far as shopping is concerned. Once the person is in the car, that means he's given up one parking space that he probably had trouble finding and he's got to go find a second parking space. If he doesn't find one quickly, the fact that he's in the car makes it very easy for him to just step on the gas, pull out of the parking lot, and go on to another shopping location that might be just a few miles down the road. It may be just a matter of a few minutes and, if you are sitting down and being propelled there, it doesn't make too much difference.

What about the lighting? Lighting is very important. Good, bright lights are very important to a center. Is the physical layout good for stores—not too many posts, good air conditioning, good heating, easy-to-read signs, well laid out parking lot, good drainage, well-maintained, attractive and appealing to the eye? All of these things are very important to making the retail property a success for the merchant and, in turn, for the landlord.

12. *Population Buying Habits.*

What are the buying habits of the population in the area? This was made reference to earlier, and is based on the age of the population—on the tastes, income level, education, types of employment, number of children, and so on. A location that is in the midst of a community with older people with few children is obviously going to cater to an entirely different kind of population area than if the people in the area are basically single-person households under the age of 25 or 30, or newly marrieds under the age of 30 without children. They have an entirely different buying habit pattern, and so what might be good for a variety store at one place won't be somewhere else. In another location, you might want to have a sporting goods shop, camera store, or beauty salon. The kind of retail store varies with the type of people you are serving in the community.

13. *Advertising.*

Lastly, you must be very concerned about advertising. Are there a number of local newspapers that cover the trade area well? You can be selling cans of coffee two for a penny but, unless you can get the word around to the community, you are not going to sell much coffee. Radio and television are basically still a little too expensive—possibly not radio, but television is too high for most retail merchants to buy—so the availability of newspapers and advertisers in the community is very important. Usually, the big metropolitan newspapers cover too large an area and, therefore, have to charge too high an advertising rate for the small- or medium-sized merchant. Also if you're in a center where there is any kind of merchant's organization, they usually promote and bring in promotional fairs, giveaways, prizes, contests, art shows, and all sorts of things to attract people. They probably also publish their own advertiser paper as a throw-away on people's lawns or mailboxes if no other publisher is taking care of this.

All of the above are important factors in determining how good a retail location might be from the point of view of investment. It might be worthwhile to say a few words about shopping centers for those of you who do have some interest in them.

Shopping Centers

Generally speaking, shopping centers are classified into three categories: the neighborhood, the community, and the regional shopping center.

1. *Neighborhood Shopping Center.*

   The neighborhood shopping center is one based around a supermarket occupying 20,000 to 25,000 square feet, doing an annual volume of at least $2 million gross. It needs usually about 10,000 people to support it, and it should have a parking ratio of about 3 or 4 square feet of parking area to every square foot of building. Ideally, there should be no other competition within 1½ to 2 miles, although this sometimes happens and some centers survive in spite of it. In addition to the supermarket, you probably have some kind of a small drug or variety store, and some various service tenants like a dry cleaner and a laundromat—things of that sort. You will not have the specialized tenants like jewelers, pet stores, and camera shops. These take larger hunks of population to support than you will find in a neighborhood shopping center, which is geared primarily to taking care of the day-to-day routine needs of the family.

2. *Community Shopping Center.*

   This is geared to handling all the retail needs of the community, but it's based on a much larger population minimum. Generally, it requires 45,000 to 50,000 people to support it and certainly should have no major competition within 3 to 5 miles. The parking ratio should be about the same as it was in the neighborhood center, and your key tenant here will be some kind of junior department store like a J. C. Penney's for example. Other tenants would include a supermarket, a drugstore, a variety store, and some clothing stores—in different price categories. A typical community shopping center would probably include a women's clothing store carrying dresses for less than $29.95, and another selling them for above $29.95; also, a shoe store, maybe a family shoe store that carries men's, women's, and children's shoes; a jeweler; a hardware store; and a variety of services, such as a barber shop, laundromat, dry cleaners, etc.

3. *Regional Shopping Center.*

   This is a giant shopping center that generally relies on somewhere around 400,000 to 500,000 people, and it is the major center for a 7- to 15-mile radius (parking ratio about the same). Your key tenant here is a major department store occupying something like 100,000 to 200,000 square feet. You would have here almost every conceivable type of tenant to satisfy the needs of a small city.

POINTS TO KEEP IN MIND

As has been said, there are a number of general factors to look at in determining how good an investment a retail store, or stores, may be. In addition to that, of course, there are specific factors that you should check out with people who are in the business to find out what makes for a good store of that kind. This check will insure you that your investment stream will not be interrupted over the years of the lease, because, again, a lease is only as good as the people who sign it and a landlord is, whether he wants to be or not, in partnership with his tenants.

$\cdots 16 \cdots$

Office Buildings

The office building is another form of attractive investment possibility. If it is done carefully, and with an understanding of what is involved in the ownership and operation of an office building, it is the type of property where management is extremely important.

Office buildings are of all types. There is the one-story, one-tenant building that you will find in some places—largely suburban areas. They range all the way up to the multistory concrete skyscraper. Generally speaking, an office building is a structure that is subdivided into small offices and houses professional people and the administrative activities of business firms. You could also include the sales activities of business firms. In order to make an intelligent investment in an office building, it is important that you consider the various factors that go into making office buildings valuable.

Value Factors

1. *Location.*

One of the most important factors of office buildings as well as retail stores, as mentioned before, is location. An office building must be in a location that will satisfy the two most important needs of the office client. These two most important needs, as far as location is concerned, are to be convenient to his customer and his employees. If your customers have to come a long distance to see you, they will very soon stop visiting you and patronize someone else who is in the same business.

Convenience is very important to customers of most office tenants. By the same token, office buildings are staffed, to a large extent, by women—secretarial help and clerks—and if it is not conveniently located for them, then you will find it difficult to recruit and maintain efficient, effective office personnel. This could seriously affect the success of the office tenant's business.

For many years, office tenants tended to locate downtown because that was convenient to their clients, but as downtown deteriorated and became less desirable to live in, they found it harder and harder to hire help. The streets weren't safe to walk; it was difficult and expensive to get there; parking—if they went by car—was expensive; the crush at peak travel hours was unbearable. So, they had to take inferior help with the result that they were losing business. Many companies that use a lot of clerical help—such as insurance companies —found that a good number of their clients were transacting their business by mail in any case, and so they began to move out toward the suburbs—out of the metropolitan areas—where it would be more convenient for the help to come to work. This is one of the reasons the people who have big real estate investments in central cities are always applying political pressure for mass rapid transit systems. Otherwise their real estate investment is going to go down the tube, as it becomes more and more unpleasant, unsafe, and difficult to work in downtown areas. The fact of the matter is that in most urban areas now, mass rapid transit is either nonexistent or very poor, and in most instances, is only designed to take care of peak-hour traffic while loading the taxpayers of the entire community with the burden of building and maintaining the system.

2. *Address.*

The address of an office building is, surprisingly, very important from the point of view of prestige. People will pay higher rent for a prestige address than they will for one that is a block away but doesn't have a prominent name. This is why people prefer to have offices on Wilshire Blvd., or Madison Ave., or Fifth Ave., as opposed to an address on Larkspur Ave. or Butterfly Lane.

3. *Groundfloor Tenant.*

As we mentioned in the case of retail tenants, the existence of a tenant with good drawing power or prestige is very important. The groundfloor tenant in an office building should be one that is very high in prestige and prominence—a bank, a stock brokerage firm, something of this sort. Attorneys, accountants, consultants, engineers, architects, all like to be in a building that has a bank on the ground floor. They certainly don't want to be in a building that has a credit dentist or a war surplus store on the ground floor. A fine restaurant, for example, might be all right, too.

4. *Appearance.*

To satisfy most tenants, the building should be elegant but conservative. Most tenants shy away from overly dramatic and far-out designs, for a variety of reasons. They are always afraid of what people will think—those who are prospective clients. Frequently, prospective clients are those with money, and they tend to be conservative. So, they're not too enamored with unusual designs in building architecture. Most clients prefer the kind of building that has a fairly simple design, clean lines, and looks attractive, elegant, and rich. Some critics, who are more inclined toward the modernistic designs, like to call it "Modern American Egg Crate." Whatever it is called, it's what sells as opposed to the wild architectural design.

5. *Public Areas.*

In keeping with the appearance, the public areas such as the lobby, hallways, stairways, and elevator cabs are very important for the impression they make on prospective tenants and on their clients— not only how these are designed and built, but how they are maintained. For example, the lobby should be spacious, well-lit, and attractive. The corridors should be the same way. Elevator cabs should have their brass or chrome fittings polished and the floors well-vacuumed or washed. When you go into a small, dingy lobby and have to ride in a rickety old elevator, you have a feeling that the building and the kind of people who occupy it are a bit threadbare.

6. *Elevators.*

In today's market, elevators are mandatory for any building over one story high. We are so spoiled today that the thought of having to walk up one flight of stairs is enough to make us go to a different attorney. Furthermore, a lot of clients who may be well-to-do are older and maybe can't manage the stairs. So, even in a two-story building, an elevator is almost a mandatory requirement for a good investment today. Whether the elevators are manned with operators or whether they are automatic is a question open to debate. Generally speaking, the automatic elevator is the most desirable. You don't have to worry about working hours or labor problems. Also, if you are talking about a building that is two or three stories high, it's possible that you could use a hydraulic elevator which has a piston on the bottom of the cab that pushes it up just like a hydraulic jack lifts a car. Unfortunately, the higher the piston moves the elevator cab the slower it goes, so that when you get to a situation where you have over two or three stories, the elevator cab moves very, very slowly which is aggravating to the people in the building and to their clients. The suspended cable, or electric elevator, is much faster but, conversely, it's much more expensive than the hydraulic elevator. However, a bad elevator service is one of the things that will drive people out of your building fairly quickly. So, it's a worthwhile expense to do it right.

7. *Air Conditioning.*

This is another very important factor, like elevators. It is as mandatory as an elevator to have air conditioning in any office building today. No matter whether it is an older building and you have to convert it, or it is a new building that you are contemplating construction of—it must have air conditioning. Now, there are various kinds of air conditioning. This is a generalized word which people really don't understand the full impact of. There are four things you can generally do with air control.

a. *Cooling*

Cooling the air is one of the things that can be done by an air conditioning unit. This is the thing that most people think of in terms of the functioning of an air conditioning unit—namely, to cool the air.

b. *Ventilation*

A second thing is ventilation. This means bringing in fresh air from the outside. This is particularly important in those kinds of buildings where you may have a lot of odors inside the building—a restaurant is a perfect case in point—where you want to introduce fresh air and take the old, stale air out.

c. *Washing or Cleaning the Air*

This is self-explanatory. You take the air and filter it or wash it before it's circulated around the building.

d. *Circulating the Air*

This simply means taking the air and moving it around. A fan will circulate the air. By moving the air in the building around, you help cool people off who are sitting in the way of the air current. If it is not planned right, it also helps give people stiff necks when the wind blows down on the back of their neck as they're sitting at their table.

Now, all air conditioning systems do some of these things, and some air conditioning systems do all of these things. Obviously, the ones that do all of these things are more expensive than the ones that do some of them. This brings up another important problem having to do with air conditioning, and that is temperature control.

8. *Temperature Control.*

A system used to control temperatures within office suites is very important. It is one of the most frequent sources of tenant complaints and there are a couple of reasons why this causes a problem. One is this: In most offices, the secretary has an inner office away from the windows and she is also the one who wears the lightest clothing of anybody in the building. The men who usually wear heavier clothing have the offices next to the windows. Whether the windows are open or not they transmit some heat from the outside, unless you have a building that has double thermal panes on the outside which is highly improbable. So, as a consequence, the gentlemen in their heavy clothes are next to the windows where it's warmest and the women with their light clothes are away—blocked off from the windows where it's coolest. Therefore, the ladies want the temperature turned up a little bit and the gentlemen want the temperature turned down a little bit. The result is that nobody's ever satisfied. This is compounded by the fact that frequently the thermostat for controlling the temperature in the office is in an entirely different suite. The reason for this is the builder or landlord was too cheap to provide zone temperature control throughout the building so that there could be a thermostat in every office suite, his thinking being that office suites change in size and layout as tenants move in and out—expand or contract. But, this is a major source of complaint and it's something you should be careful of when you buy or erect a building.

9. *Heating.*

There are various ways of heating a building. What is being discussed is the same sort of thing as air conditioning, but it is the heating of air inside the office. In this regard, it's handy to know that generally the use of several different kinds of fuel and various kinds of carriers of the heat are being talked about. In terms of fuel, either coal, oil, natural gas, or, to a limited extent, electricity is being referred to. This is what produces the heat.

The agent used to carry heat to the various rooms is either air, such as in a forced-air system; steam, such as in a steam radiator system, where we have hot steam going through the radiator which throws off heat into the room; or water, such as burying coils of water pipes in the floor of a room and pushing the water, at the right temperature, through these coils. The water system is not in widespread use today. Mostly steam or air systems are used in heating large buildings.

The same problem of temperature control is important here because the thermostat may very well be hooked up to both the air conditioner and the heat. You may have what is called a heat pump which both heats and cools the air. So far, the heat pump is regarded as less costly to install but more expensive to keep up because it has so many electrical relays that must be maintained. Its general use to date has been limited to smaller buildings and, because it has been in existence for less than ten years, it is not regarded as a tried, true, and tested approach. However, I think it has some great possibilities.

10. *Parking.*

Adequate parking for both tenants, their employees, and their clients is critical. This is becoming increasingly important as more people find public transportation is inadequate and, with the exception of some really downtown locations around the country, the car has become the primary source of transportation for most people—be they tenants, or employees, or their clients. The amount of parking, the ease of getting in and out, is all critically important and can make the difference between a successful and an unsuccessful building. The same guide patterns should be followed in determining parking as was mentioned in the chapter on retail stores when I discussed effective parking. I have never encountered an office building that had too much effective parking. There is no such thing as having too much of this. There *is*, however, such a thing as having too much ineffective parking, because it's expensive and nobody uses it. If you are going to charge for parking, there should be some way for the client to get it back on a validation system from the tenant. You should be able to get it back from the tenant either one way or another—through validation, higher rent, or something of that sort.

11. *Tenants.*

There are very few large office buildings constructed on pure speculation, because it just doesn't work out. Most of them are partially preleased to larger tenants. We have the same kind of situation here as we have with retail store arrangement—with a shopping center. The institution that lends the money for the building relies a good deal on the credit of the tenant. It's concerned with the amount, length, and stability of the income streams that the leases are going to generate. So these are very important—good, long-term leases. Now, there is one theory that claims it's better to have a building sit vacant for a year than to make any concessions or compromises necessary to attract clients. There is another theory that says it's better to have a building leased up, even if you don't make any money for a year.

I'm a firm believer in the second theory. I know, for example, one office building manager who takes over a new building and immediately begins canvassing all the office buildings in the area for tenants. This is, obviously, after the major tenant has been selected and a lease signed with the tenant so the building can be erected. For filling up the rest of the building, he canvasses every other tenant in the neighborhood—wherever his building is located—and calls to inquire if they would be interested in moving into a brand new building. He is willing to make all kinds of concessions to get that tenant out of his old building and into the new one. For example, if the tenant in the old building says he has two years left to go on his present lease, the manager will take over that lease for him. Then he can move into the new building immediately. If the tenant says he doesn't want to bother with the expense of moving, the manager offers to move him into the new building at no expense and throw in a color television set as a little extra sweetener. If the tenant says the rent is too high, the manager tells him he can move into the building and sign a lease, then the rent will start only after he has been in the building for a certain amount of time. Therefore, the average rent over the term of occupancy will be at a price the tenant is willing to pay, even though the rent he pays during the term of the lease will be the price the landlord feels is necessary to make the building pay for itself. In other words, the landlord might move the tenant in and give him 11 years occupancy of the building but have him signed to a lease on a ten-year basis. The rate that the tenant pays in the ten years is the rate that the landlord wants to collect to make the building a success. However, by giving the tenant 11 years occupancy, the tenant is getting it for his price, too.

At the end of the first six months, the manager or owner of the building in case number one can only tell the bank that he doesn't have any tenants in the building but is hopeful he'll get some soon. In the second case (using the theory of filling the building by merchandising the space, instead of sitting there demanding that everybody meet his terms), the landlord is able to tell the bank that he is positive the money will start coming in six months from now, because he has the building leased and occupied. That could be the difference between the success or failure of a building.

Now, if you, as an investor, are buying a new building, it's important that you know when such concessions have been made. I think I've made it clear that I don't think there is anything wrong with concessions as such, because without them a lot of buildings would go bankrupt. I also think that going bankrupt is a lot worse for a property than making some concessions. However, if you are going to invest in such a property, you should find out what concessions have been made so that you know what it is you're buying. In other words, if you are going to buy a building that has a year's free rent billed into the first 11 years of its income stream, then you want to pay a price that is predicated on the actual income stream over that 11 years and *not* the paper income stream based on ten years. The reason for this is that when the old ten-year lease is up, the tenants may come to you and say that to renew they want the same kind of deal they had when they moved in—a year's free rent to sign a ten-year lease, or whatever.

Another factor that's very important to realize about tenants is that you have to be careful about the types you let into your building, because some tenants will drive others away. The groundfloor tenant was discussed earlier in the chapter, but that isn't the only example. For instance, professional workers in many offices don't want to be associated with anything that is slightly on the periphery of the business operation—that has anything less than the same kind of prestige that they as tenants, themselves, enjoy. For this reason, attorneys, architects, engineers, and professional men of all kinds may be reluctant to work in a building that houses nonprofessional activities.

12. *Area Measurement.*

It is important to understand how most office buildings measure the area of their building in terms of what they are renting to a tenant because, here again, if you don't understand it, you might get taken. Generally speaking, when a building is planned, it is presumed that it will earn a certain amount of money in order to get the kind of return necessary on the investment. This would be sufficient return to pay off the mortgage as well as bring the investor a return on his equity. Most offices are rented on some kind of square-footage basis founded on this projection of income. The rent can be quoted as either so many cents per square foot per month or so many dollars per square foot per year. It really doesn't make any difference how you express it as long as it comes out the same way.

Now, in terms of measuring the area of a subdivided floor of an office building (by subdivided, I mean a floor that is divided into offices for more than one tenant), you will not charge the tenant for the public area—the corridors, the elevators, the lobby, the stairways, etc.—

although actually, in a sense, you are charging him because even though you leave these things out of your calculations, you are going to have to raise your rent accordingly to cover the cost of these parts of the building. However, that is neither here nor there. Technically, you are charging only for the space actually occupied. And, the most common way of estimating the space is to measure from the inside of exterior building walls to the public side of corridor, lobby, or other public area walls, and from the center of party walls to the center of adjacent party walls. (A party wall is the wall between two adjoining tenants' offices.)

If one tenant comes along and takes an entire floor, you can very magnanimously let him have the entire floor for less than the average square foot rental of offices which are subdivided. The reasoning behind this is that he is going to be taking what would have been the corridor, or hallway, or floor lobby area, etc., so that by taking over more square footage than would be normal if the floor was divided up among several tenants, you can give it to him for less per square foot. You are still going to get the same amount of dollars per floor no matter how you slice it. If you don't, you're in trouble.

13. *Management.*

The successful operation of an office building depends on management more than anything else. A professional manager knows the market. He knows how to lease the building aggressively; how to manage it; how to preserve the most beneficial ratio of incoming rents to outgoing expenses. And, he also knows how to deal with tenants courteously, understandingly, sympathetically, and firmly. If you are going to make a success of an office building operation in a highly competitive market—and that is what most urban areas are today— you are going to have to utilize professional management that doesn't make mistakes. I have seen office buildings owned by major insurance companies which they think they can manage themselves. These firms do a terrible, botched-up job of it and, as a result, lose lots of money on their investment because the building sits vacant too long.

One of the most common mistakes made is to wait until a building is finished and standing there vacant before calling in a professional building manager.

The building manager should be brought in before the first line is drawn on a piece of paper by the architect. The manager is the man who can test the market. He knows what the market is for office space. He knows what is renting these days. He knows what people are looking for and what is important to have in the building. He should be in on planning from the very first day. The result will be a much higher profit for the investor.

Some Random Points

1. Efficiency.

There are a few other random points I should mention before we leave the subject of office buildings. One is the term "efficiency." You will frequently hear people talking about how efficient an office building is. Efficiency refers to the ratio of rentable square footage in the building relative to the total square footage. The more efficient the building, the higher the ratio is of rentable square footage to total square footage. For example, if a building is 85% efficient, that means 85% of the total square footage in the building will produce some kind of rental income. I would make the point that, as a general rule, a building under 80% efficiency is a very suspicious investment. Eighty per cent efficiency is about the bottom level that should be reached. If it's less than this, it means that 1 foot out of every 5 feet is not paying its way. Another point I consider very important for most investors to keep in mind is "building experience exchanges."

2. Building Experience Exchanges.

Both the Building Owners and Managers Association and the Institute of Real Estate Management have, from time to time, "office building experience exchanges." These are surveys that they make of office buildings around the country, and they indicate what the cost should be for various aspects of operating the building. This gives you a good comparison rule to see whether your building, or the building you're contemplating buying, is functioning the way it should be. For example, let's say that you look at an office building exchange that says painting and redecorating should take 9% of the gross income, and when you look at the books of the building you're contemplating buying, you find that painting and decorating are taking up 18%.

Seeing this great variance between what other buildings are paying for painting and decorating and what the building you're looking at is paying, should set off an alarm bell that there is something wrong with the building or the way it's managed. Either way, it's to the detriment of your investment dollar. Finally, let's make an observation about how different people appraise the value of office buildings.

3. How Much Is It Worth?

There can be no question that the most important and soundest way of appraising an office building is by the so-called "income approach." You are interested in what the net income of the building is—what it can generate, in terms of net income, every year. What it costs to create is of no concern at all. Just because the architect, the engineer, the developer, and the lender have allowed a Taj Mahal white elephant to become encased in concrete and steel does not mean that you should use your investment dollars to bail them out of their mistake.

The cost of creating an office building is of no consequence at all. The important thing is what kind of net income it will produce. If it produces zero net income, then the building is worth nothing even if it cost $1 billion to construct. If it produces $100,000 a year net income and you assume an investment return of 10%, it is worth $1 million. It's as simple as that. Yet, curiously enough, bankers too often rely on the cost of creating the building as a basis for judging its value. Let's hope that you, as an investor, are smarter than the foolish bankers who rely on this.

POINTS TO KEEP IN MIND

Some of the things that make value in office building property are:

- *Location.*
- *Address.*
- *Groundfloor tenant.*
- *Appearance.*
- *Condition of public areas.*
- *Elevators.*
- *Air conditioning and heating.*
- *Parking.*
- *Other tenants.*
- *Management.*

Some other points to remember include:

- *How office space is measured.*
- *Building efficiency.*
- *Building experience exchanges.*

···17···

Investing in
Industrial Real Estate

Industrial property can be both a good and a troublesome investment. Long and involved books have been written about industrial property, but I'll try to cover the most important points for the average investor in just this one chapter.

What Is Industrial Property?

As usual, before talking too much about any particular kind of investment, it's helpful to know what it is. There are various ways of defining industrial property. One description, used by some people, is that it is property zoned for industrial use by a local planning commission and/or zoning board. Another definition might be that it is any kind

187

of property, improved or unimproved, that is used for any kind of industrial use.

When you stop and consider the various kinds of industrial uses there are, you can see right away that you face scores of different types of property that might be classified as industrial. Each one of these could be markedly different from any other industrial property. After all, industrial activities include such diverse things as: mining, refining, fabricating and assembling products, power plants, steel mills, warehouses, truck terminals, loft buildings, little automobile garages, giant sawmills, freight yards, loading and unloading docks, watchmaking firms, atomic energy plants, and so on.

Of course, the average investor is highly unlikely to buy an atomic energy plant or a railroad yard, so those won't be covered in this chapter. In fact, the discussion will deal with generalized observations and factors affecting the value of industrial real estate rather than any particular type of industrial property.

VALUE FACTORS

There are a number of factors which affect the value of industrial property generally, and in the next few paragraphs those will be used as a broad guide for what to look for when considering industrial property as an investment.

Special-Use Design

Improved industrial property is designed to meet the specialized needs of a particular type of industrial activity. Each particular kind of industrial activity—be it bottling beer, assembling automobiles, mining copper, refining oil, or whatever—requires a particular kind of building layout: height, width, shape, and so on. In fact, many companies in the same line of business have different physical plant requirements because of their particular patented processes or methods of creating or fabricating their particular product.

There is nothing wrong with a specially designed building or improvement except that, generally speaking, it is not adaptable to the requirements of some other tenant in the event the original tenant decides to move out. So, if you are buying a building that has been designed for a particular kind of tenant, you must recognize that when and if that tenant moves out of the building, you could be faced with a very expensive remodeling problem. In fact, there is the possibility that you may not be able to use the improvement at all, and you should bear this in mind when you buy this building or construct it, in terms of what kind of a return you want on your investment.

High Obsolescence Rate

In keeping with what was just mentioned about the special-purpose nature of many industrial buildings, these kinds of buildings have a high obsolescence rate. That means that they wear out or become obsolete much sooner than an ordinary building. The building may physically still be standing and in good condition, but as far as its usefulness as an industrial building is concerned it may be completely obsolete.

Now, this is not just because of its special-design nature or because a tenant for whom the building was originally built has vacated it. It may be that the same tenant remains in the building but because of advances in technology, the way that he goes about manufacturing or placing his particular product changes radically from the norm in a period of four or five years.

A friend of mine at General Electric recently told me that his company now makes 80% of their profit from products that weren't even invented ten years ago! Now, most people in the industrial world will tell you that, unless a company keeps ahead of its field by constant research and innovation and changing its methods and systems, it is going to lose ground with its competitors and ultimately end up in the red.

Very well, this may be fine on the one hand; however, it wreaks havoc with improved industrial real estate because it means constantly changing designs to accommodate new processings, new techniques, and new technology. And, here again, you will be writing off the original investment in the building at a faster rate than you would do if you were just concerning yourself with the physical depreciation of the building.

Client Location Factors

There are a great many factors that affect the decision of an industrial firm to locate their plant in any given place. Because of the variety of manufacturing activities that there are, as discussed earlier, I will only be able to speak in generalized terms. But, these should be most helpful to the average investor in terms of deciding whether the industrial property that he is contemplating buying is really a property that is attractive and desirable to prospective tenants or, for that matter, prospective industrial buyers. Because, if the property isn't attractive to a potential buyer then the average investor or, for that matter, any investor, is not going to be able to make a profit. It's the old supply and demand rule again.

1. *Labor.*

Labor is one of the most important factors connected with any business operation, including those firms that are in industry. You must be located at a place where you can get people with the right kinds of skills who are willing to work for the right kind of money, if you are going to be able to function. Let's consider some examples of what this means.

The state of California produces some of the finest long-staple cotton in the country. For many years now, California has been among the top two or three cotton producers in the United States. Most of this cotton is grown in the central valley of California which is located 100 miles north of Los Angeles. Now, Los Angeles is also a great fabric-consuming city, since it is probably the second largest fashion center in the United States. It would seem logical, therefore, that cotton that is grown in central California should be woven into cloth in California and shipped 100 miles to Los Angeles for its consumption.

In fact, this is not what happens. What actually happens is that the cotton grown in California is shipped across the entire United States to South Carolina, North Carolina, and some of the other southern states. There it is woven into cloth. Then, the finished cloth is shipped back across the entire United States to Los Angeles where it is ultimately used for suits, dresses, swimming apparel, and other types of clothing. The reason for this strange arrangement requiring the shipment of cotton some 6,000 miles in order to travel a net distance of 100, is labor. Southern California does not have the quantities of skilled labor that are willing to work for the low wages that people in cotton mills are accustomed to paying.

You have other anomalies that allow German firms to buy aluminum ore in Galveston, Texas; ship it back to Hamburg, Germany; make it into pots and pans there; ship it back to Galveston, Texas; and sell the pots and pans for less money than the people who manufacture the pots and pans in Texas are able to.

The same thing occurs with the Japanese who are able to import cotton from India; weave it into cloth; ship it back to India; and then sell it for less money than the Indians are able to. The common factor here is the availability of cheap, skilled labor.

Now the labor need not necessarily be cheap; it may be just a matter of its availability. Many aerospace firms seeking highly skilled engineers locate in areas where engineers are abundant. And, these are not inexpensive people; it just so happens that engineers prefer to be located in urban areas near places where they can get the kind of education for their children that they want; live in the kind of neighborhoods they like; advance their own education by attending universities and colleges; and have access to good recreational and cultural activities.

This is why you don't see many engineering plants located in North Dakota, for example, or Mississippi. You find that most plants engaging highly skilled engineers are located near urban areas—Southern California, the Houston area of Texas, Boston, New York State, and so on.

2. *Transportation.*

Transportation is another important factor, obviously. If you can't bring the raw materials to your industrial plant and ship the finished goods out from your industrial plant, then you will have a warehouse full of beautiful industrial goods that everybody wants to buy but nobody can get. Years back, when people talked about transportation for industrial plants, the first thing that jumped into their minds was railroad lines or water transport of some kind. This is not the case anymore because of the great expansion of roads and truck facilities, as well as the fact that a lot of the more expensive items that are sold by some manufacturers are small in size and light in weight, and now can be transported quickly anyplace in the world by air. In fact, wealthy nations have gotten to the point now where they even ship missiles by air. So, air freight is a growing thing.

But, all that notwithstanding, transportation is an important factor in making an industrial site desirable; and, from the point of view of the investor—therefore profitable. The availability of raw materials is another very important characteristic of an industrial site. Obviously, it is an advantage for a manufacturer to be close to the site of his raw materials. This cuts down on transportation charges. By the same token, it is important for an industrial firm to be convenient to the market in which it wishes to sell its end product. So, ideally, an industrial client would like to locate centrally to both its raw materials and the market for its end product.

An example of how this can be done is Gary, Indiana. The important steel mills were built in Gary because it was convenient to the raw materials necessary to make steel. Cheap water transportation brings iron ore from the Mesabi Range in Northern Minnesota through the Great Lakes to the shores of Gary. Relatively cheap rail transportation brings coal from nearby Pennsylvania coal fields. And, the third important raw material for the making of steel—limestone—is native to

Indiana. While, on the other side of the picture, Gary is conveniently located near some of the main consumers of steel—for example, the automobile industry in Detroit, Michigan.

3. *Utilities.*

Other factors that are of importance in selecting industrial sites are the availability and cost of utilities. For example, if you were going to locate a brewery, you would want it to be conveniently near large supplies of water and a good sewer system, because breweries use and throw off a lot of water.

4. *Politics.*

Your local political situation (as far as unions are concerned), taxes, and receptivity to industry are all very important. Many times, a community will build roads and a lot of other facilities to bring industry into it, as well as forestall taxes for years to come. This can be very important from the profit point of view of the industrialist and obviously makes the property in that community far more attractive; therefore, it is important from the point of view of the real estate investor. Another factor is the question of employees' amenities: Is it a pleasant place to live? Does it have opportunities for cultural advantages?— whatever it is that attracts employees of that particular industry.

5. *Recreation.*

You will find, for example, that industries largely staffed by so-called blue collar workers are interested in sports and recreational facilities. They like to be located in a town where there's a major league baseball or football team. They would like to be in a place where it's convenient to go fishing, hunting, boating, and so on. On the other hand, employees who have gone on to advanced education are interested in being closer to urban areas where there are more cultural facilities available—the opera, the ballet, the legitimate theatre, libraries, advanced universities.

6. *Advanced Education.*

Many engineers, for example, and scientists, too, want to be in a community where they can pursue their education. As an example, a man may have a Masters Degree in Engineering or a Bachelors Degree in Engineering but he wants to go after a PhD; therefore, he will make sacrifices in the kind of job he gets and the salary he accepts, if necessary, as long as he can pursue his work toward his PhD. This will ultimately be important to him and he will subsequently be paid back in higher wages. All of these things—labor, transportation, raw materials, availability, and receptivity—are very important in determining where an industrial plant will be located. They are not, however, the only factors, and many of these factors will vary in importance from industry to industry.

Lack of Speculative Value

Industrial improvements are rarely done on a speculative basis because of the high obsolescence rate discussed earlier and the special-use design. While you will find builders and real estate investors who will raise tracts of houses, apartment buildings, or shopping centers on a speculative basis—that is, they will build without having tenants for all of the property available at the time they begin construction—this is rarely the case in an industrial property. You don't know what the tenant's requirements are until you've got him signed on the dotted line; therefore, you don't know what to build. So much of improved industrial property is tailor-made to the specific tenant that it is virtually impossible to build speculative industrial buildings.

This is not to say that it isn't done. There are certain types of buildings which lend themselves to speculative construction such as the row-upon-row garage, stall-type industrial building for small tenants, or the large, loft-type building or warehouse where the tenant that would normally take that space just wants four walls and a roof in any case— and it's not an assembly or manufacturing plant.

But, for so many of the other kinds of industrial improvements, it is impossible to build until you have a specific tenant in mind. This relates strongly to the next factor that should be considered.

Long Vacancy Period

Traditionally, industrial properties, when they become vacant, remain vacant longer than any other kind of property. The reasons for this should be self-evident by this time. The special-use design, the high obsolescence rate, the high cost of rebuilding to suit a tenant—all these things may be beyond the average investor's capabilities. So that while it may be unusual for an apartment, a home, a store, or an office to remain vacant for more than a few months, it is not unusual for an industrial building to remain vacant for months and months—and even years. This is something that must be taken into consideration in determining the soundness of any kind of industrial property as an investment. And, of course, these factors which affect the return to the investor are also ones which affect the attitudes of lenders on industrial property, which will be discussed next.

Lenders' Reluctance

Lenders are very reluctant to accept the real estate security for their loans. They are aware of all the factors spoken of so far, and this makes them very chary of undertaking heavy mortgage obligations in industrial property. They are aware of the special-use design, the obsolescence rate problem, the lack of speculative value, the difficulty in finding tenants for a building that is unoccupied. So, while you can go to a lender and talk in terms of the cost of producing an apartment building and use that as a basis on which to borrow construction funds and permanent financing, this is of little value in persuading a banker to lend money to you on an industrial building. He realizes that if you don't get a good tenant for the building, or if there are changes in the technology of the industry, he might be lucky as a banker to bail out 50¢ on the dollar in terms of recovering value for his mortgage. This leads into the main consideration that bankers have in lending on industrial property, which is discussed next.

Credit Standing of the Tenant

No single factor is more important to the banker and to the investor than the credit standing of the tenant. Here, again, we must look to all the things that we have scrutinized before in terms of analyzing the stability of the tenant. What the lender is lending on and what the investor is investing on with regard to an industrial property is more often than not the income stream generated by that tenant. This means you must look at the income stream and see how secure it is. How likely is it that the tenant will pay it off for the term he's obligated to under the terms of the lease? Remember, a lease is only as good as the people that sign it. So a long lease with a financially unstable firm really is kind of meaningless, because they can go bankrupt tomorrow and you can whistle for your money. The ideal situation is, of course, to have a long lease with a very firm, financially sold tenant paying a good rate of return. And, of course, there are many factors to concern yourself with in terms of the lease, but those will be covered in Chapter 20.

POINTS TO KEEP IN MIND

~~~~~~

Value factors in industrial property are:

- *Special-use design.*
- *High obsolescence rate.*
- *Client location factors.*

  –Labor.
  –Transportation.
  –Utilities.
  –Politics.
  –Recreation.
  –Advanced education.

- *Lack of speculative value.*
- *Long vacancy period.*
- *Lender's reluctance.*
- *Tenant's credit standing.*

VI

REAL ESTATE INVESTMENTS
AND INCOME TAXES

···18···

Benefiting from Income Taxes

===============

    A major benefit of owning real estate is the tax advantages that go along with it. Of primary concern are federal income taxes, although state income taxes are also of some importance.

    Real estate is a good tax shelter. However, you must understand what it's all about in order to use the advantages built into the Internal Revenue Code for your personal profit.

    Unfortunately, there are too many myths and confusions floating around about how real estate can or cannot be used to save on income taxes. Sad to report, they are often perpetrated by well-meaning but badly informed real estate salesmen. When in doubt, see a good real estate tax man. It's worth it.

    Meanwhile, here are same of the tax advantages of owning real estate:

1. *Profit as a Capital Gain.*

A profit can be a capital gain; whereas, a loss can be an ordinary loss. That is to say, when you make a profit on the sale of your property, you can consider it as a capital gain. As you know, this reduces the amount of income tax you must pay. On the other hand, if you have a loss from the sale of real estate, you may often deduct the full amount of the loss from your ordinary income.

2. *Spreading the Profit.*

Another advantage is that the profit may be spread. You can do this through an installment sale. It might not be advantageous for you to take all of your profit this year, or even next year. You can spread it out over a number of years through the use of an installment sale.

3. *Repair and Maintenance.*

Repair and maintenance on investment type real estate and income real estate may be deducted.

4. *Casualty Losses.*

A casualty loss is deductible. If you have a loss from some kind of a casualty, like a fire, flood, or windstorm, you can deduct whatever amount the insurance company doesn't pay you. The insurance company will rarely pay you 100 cents on the dollar for your loss. They don't like to do that because of the so-called "moral hazard." If you were paid 100 cents on the dollar for your loss, there might be a temptation to stage an accident. Inasmuch as the insurance company does not pay you for the total loss you sustain from a casualty source, then you may deduct the difference from your income tax.

5. *Tenant Improvements.*

The improvements of a tenant to your property are yours tax free. Sometimes you don't want them, but they are tax free to you. The effect of this is that often a tenant wants air conditioning put in or, perhaps, new carpeting. The landlord tells the tenant to put it in, and he will deduct it from the rent. While the landlord is technically paying for it, he's not getting rent on which he has to pay income tax. In addition, he would probably have to capitalize the cost of that improvement if he paid for it directly. That is, he'd have to spread out the life of that improvement over the life of the building. Therefore, he wouldn't be able to charge off the full amount in the year that he paid it out. Consider an improvement that costs $1,000 in a building with 20 years of life left. If the landlord pays for the improvement directly, he can usually only deduct $50 a year. If the tenant pays for it and deducts it from the rent, the landlord has the improvement made plus $1,000 less income to pay tax on to the government.

6. *Custody and Control.*

Custody and control of the property by lease or purchase. There aren't very many things in our present economic system that we own outright as such. Most of the things that we have are in a partnership with the bank or the finance company. The important thing is not really whether you own it, but whether you have custody and control of it. In other words, you don't really care who *owns* your house or who actually *owns* your car. What you care about is that you have the exclusive right to *use* those things.

Suppose you see a piece of property that you'd like to buy. Then, suppose the owner doesn't want to sell it because he faces a tremendous income tax problem. He bought it in 1903 for $84, and today it is worth $100,000. He doesn't want to sell it and pay that tremendous tax. Yet, you want that property. So you suggest that he lease it to you for 55 years. If you have an exclusive lease for 55 years, you have the full right to use of the property even to the exclusion of the owners.

Admittedly, the lease will cost you more money over the term of 55 years, yet it costs you less money at the beginning to gain control of it. It will take some years before you will have paid out the full price. And, somewhere along the line you may sell the lease. There is a growing market in leases on valuable pieces of property.

a. *Financing Leasehold Improvements*

The big difficulty with leasing is that of financing improvements. If you're leasing raw land, the financing can become very difficult. Unless the landlord will subordinate his lease, you may have to pay for all the improvements in cash. Usually the building represents the biggest share of the total property value. For example, take a situation where the building-to-land ratio is 2:1. This means the building is worth twice what the land is worth. If you lease the land, you will put up twice as much cash in the project. This is because your cash is going into the improvements instead of the land. However, there are ways of getting around this. One way is to get the owner of the leased land to subordinate (or take a position junior to a construction loan) his lease.

b. *One Solution*

Many institutions will not lend money on a building unless the lease is subordinated. They are afraid that the land tenant (to whom they have lent construction money) may default on his lease. The land owner may then declare the ground lease in default and take over the ground. When he takes over the ground, he is in effect taking over the building, too. Since the leasing of land is becoming more important, many approaches are being explored to deal with the problem. For example, here is one method that often succeeds in getting the landowner to subordinate the land.

If the landowner will sign a lease with you for 55 years, you will then go to, say, New York Life Insurance for a loan. New York Life says it will lend you the money to build on this property, but doesn't want to take the chance that you'll default on the land-lease payments. The insurance company wants the right to cure any default in the lease. This means that if you default on your land-rent payment to the landlord of the land, the insurance company can step in and make those land-rent payments.

You then go back to the landowner and ask if he will agree to subordinate if there is a cosignatory (the insurance company) on the land lease. Most people will agree because they now have a major financial institution standing behind their land leases. Under this arrangement, the lease usually has a clause stating that the lease is automatically assigned to the financial institution that lends money on the improvement if there is a default on the land lease.

The owner of the land has you signed on the lease and, if you don't pay, he can turn to the lender. The lender is happy because it knows that nothing can happen to take the ground out from under the building during the term of the mortgage.

Usually all the improvements revert to the owner of the land at the end of the lease. This may be good or bad for the landowner. It depends on the kind of improvements that have been made. If it's a very substantial building, it will still have some value at the end of the lease. However, most developers work it so the building isn't worth much at the end of the lease.

7. *Best Title Advantage.*

The title may be taken in the best tax way for the owner. You don't have to take title in your own name. You can take title in the name of a corporation, in joint tenancy, or in the name of a trustee. You can take it any way you want that is best for you.

Consider this situation: You happen to be a developer, and you're making lots of money. You're in a high income tax bracket. There is a property that is going to be very good—very lucrative for you—and you want to buy it. But, one of the things that holds you back is that most of the profit you're going to make on this property will go to taxes. You may decide to take the title to this in the name of a corporation, in order to have a lower tax rate. You may want to take it in the name of one of your infant children. His tax rate is probably lower than yours. Of course, you'll have to file a separate tax return for him, and you won't be able to claim the $600 deduction. Even so, you probably end up with more net income after taxes.

8. *Advantageous Tax Elections.*

You may elect to deduct or capitalize interest, taxes, etc. on nonproductive property. For example, if you own a piece of property that you purchased for investment purposes—not income property—you can either deduct the costs of caring for and protecting this property while you hold it, or you can let it accumulate and deduct it all at one time. You can deduct it in the year that is most advantageous to you.

For example, if you buy 10 acres of land, you have to consider what it is going to cost you in terms of paying interest on the mortgage, the taxes, and so on. You may have to protect the land from erosion and floods. Now, suppose in the year you do this, all of these things add up to $5,000. You can elect to either deduct that total $5,000 in this year; carry this over for ten years and deduct $500 a year; or you might let it accumulate. When you sell it, that $5,000 is part of the cost of holding the property. So whatever is the best thing for you from a tax point of view, you may do. This also includes money you may have to spend to protect your title to the property. If somebody sues you, contending that it really isn't your property, you have to defend your title to the property.

Tax Categories

Real estate is categorized by Internal Revenue in five different ways:

1. *Personal Residence.*

One category is your personal home. You may have only one personal home at a time. It must be the place which is your principal residence most of the time. On your personal home, you may not deduct depreciation or the expenses of operating a home. You can't deduct all the things you can from income property, such as maintenance and repair. You can deduct taxes and the interest on your mortgage.

2. *Property Held for Sale.*

Another category is property that is held for sale to customers. If you are a dealer in real estate, you purchase real estate and hold it for sale to other people. Or, you may buy raw land, subdivide it, and sell off the lots. If you are a dealer, you are not entitled to tax deductions for such things as repair and maintenance or operating expenses.

3. *Investment Property.*

This is property that is held for investment. This does not produce income, but it is held for some future purpose, such as appreciation in price or speculation.

4. *Income Property.*

As the name implies, this is property that produces income. It may be commercial, or residential, or any kind of income property.

5. *Business Property.*

The last category is business property. This is property used in your trade and business. You may deduct the expenses of operating these properties, including repair and maintenance.

Tax Differences Among Categories

The biggest difference between the personal home and property held for sale to customers, is the tax on the profit when you sell it. You can't claim a capital gains tax on property held for sale to customers when you're a dealer in real estate. Your personal home is an entirely different ball of wax. You may or may not have to pay a capital gain tax on any profit. It depends on whether or not you buy another home and for what price. You can get the capital gains advantage when you sell the speculation property and make a profit on it.

Who Is a Dealer?

Who is a dealer? That is something that the Internal Revenue Service decides. Of course in case of disputes, the ultimate decision is made by the Tax Court. However, if you follow the general guidelines that Internal Revenue sets down, you will probably get along without much trouble.

If you deal in real estate as a regular business—have an office where you buy, sell, and subdivide real estate—then you're a dealer. If you do not regularly buy and sell real estate, but just do it occasionally, then you're probably not a dealer.

No one of these things is a sure test. You can sell a piece of property and not be a dealer if you can prove that you don't customarily do this sort of thing. However, if you put signs up, list property with brokers, have an office where you buy and sell land all the time, run ads in the paper, and do things that make the property more saleable, then you will probably be classified as a dealer. This means that all the profits you make must be reported as ordinary income rather than capital gain.

This is why some people buy acreage to hold for subdivision, but will not do the subdividing themselves. They won't put in the streets, sidewalks, curbs, sewers, and streetlights. They are afraid this will put them in the category of being a dealer. If these improvements are done by someone other than the owner, he may avoid being considered a dealer.

Your Residence

A few words about your personal home. You can avoid paying tax on the sale of your home, even if it is more than what you paid for it originally. If there is a profit in the sale of your personal home, you pay no tax on that profit if you buy another home within one year (before or after) the sale. Your new home must cost at least as much as you got for the old home. I don't mean necessarily in terms of cash, but in terms of the total prices.

For example, you might sell your old home for $25,000, with $5,000 cash down payment and buy another home for $28,000 with $2,000 cash down payment. You end up with $3,000 cash but with no tax liability. The test is that you bought your new home for $28,000 and sold the old one for $25,000. Therefore, there is no taxable income generated.

Before and After

If the new home is being built for you rather than being an existing home, you have a year and a half after the sale of the old home to take possession. When you're buying an existing home, you can buy it a year *before* or a year *after*. However, if a home is being built for you, you have only a year and a half after. They don't give you any time before.

The reason for the before provision with an existing new home is fairly logical. You might decide to sell your old home and go looking for a new one. Suppose you find a new home that you desire. You don't want to lose that new home, so you buy the new home before you've actually sold the old home. It might be two, three, or four months before the old home sells, so you're allowed the year before and the year after.

After Only

If the new house is to be built, you have exactly a year and a half. The year-and-a-half rule has been very rigidly enforced. Strikes, walkouts, or shortages of materials are not taken into consideration. The cutoff time is exactly 18 months after you've sold the old home.

I recall one case that went to the Tax Court. Because of materials shortage, the new home that was being built was not completed within the year and a half allowed. There was another month to go to complete the house when the 18 months ran out. The Tax Court held that the value of the new home had to be established as of its work at that point in construction.

Home or Income Property?

Suppose you buy a new house before you've sold the old one, and move into the new house. If you convert the old home into income property, you can enjoy the tax advantages of the income property category. However, you've got to prove that you have either converted the old house into income property or made a conscientious effort to do so. For example, you should offer the old house for rent at a reasonable rental and do whatever is reasonably necessary to rent the house. You'd put up a "For Rent" sign, run ads in the paper, and list it with a rental broker. Even if you didn't succeed in renting, the house should then qualify as income property.

If, on the other hand, you offer it for rent at a purposely outrageous price, or don't advertise and try to rent it, the property will probably not qualify as income property.

POINTS TO KEEP IN MIND

Some of the tax and financial advantages of real estate investment are:

- *Profits can be capital gain.*
- *Profits can be spread.*
- *Repair and maintenance is deductible.*
- *Casualty losses are deductible.*
- *Tenant improvements are tax-free gain in property's value.*
- *Custody and control of property don't depend on ownership.*
- *Title may be held in the most advantageous way.*
- *The method of taxation may be chosen by the taxpayer to his advantage.*

Tax categories of real estate include:

- *Personal residence.*
- *Property held for sale.*
- *Investment property.*
- *Income property.*
- *Business property.*

···19···

Depreciation and
Other Tax Deductions

━━━━━━━━━━━━━━━━━━

One of the biggest tax savings real estate can offer the investor is through depreciation. This chapter will explore that aspect in detail, along with some other tax-saving devices.

What Is Depreciation?

Depreciation is simply "a loss in value." There are three kinds of depreciation: economic depreciation, functional depreciation, and physical depreciation. Physical depreciation is the most common. You'll chiefly be concerned with physical depreciation, although these other two categories are also very important.

Economic Depreciation

Economic depreciation is a loss in demand for a particular property, or a loss in value because the demand for a property has gone down due to some external cause. It may be something that has nothing to do with the property itself, but with economic conditions. If a major company loses a big government contract, thousands of people may be laid off. There is a loss in value to all the properties in the area. This may result in economic depreciation in property.

When a freeway opens up and cuts off a lot of business, some suffer and some prosper because of it. The properties that suffer lose value because of economic depreciation. In other words, a businessman who is running a gas station and a coffee shop that depends on transient trade, may go broke because the freeway bypasses him. On the other hand, with heavy traffic gone from this street, it may become a prime site for an apartment house. It depends on the situation.

The announcement that a developer is going to build a shopping center across the street is not a case of economic depreciation, it is a case of economic *appreciation*. Conversely, announcement that a chicken-fat packaging plant will go in next door would be a case of economic depreciation.

Functional Depreciation

Functional depreciation is a loss in value due to something that is inherent in the property. In the case of a single-family home, it could be a poor layout in the house. You may have to go through two bedrooms to get to a bathroom. A bizarre architectural style that is not appealing to the general public would be a handicap. You must deduct some value because it doesn't have appeal for a broad market. Inadequate mechanical equipment is another cause of functional loss in value. For example, a brand new $60,000 house with no garbage disposal, built-ins, or inside plumbing is a dramatic example of functional depreciation.

Most people think solely of physical depreciation, and only in terms of older houses. It is possible for a brand new house to have functional depreciation. The example just given is an illustration of functional depreciation in a new house.

Physical Depreciation

Physical depreciation is a loss in value due to action of the elements; wear and tear; use of the improvements; or, structural ageing. A building gets old and begins to creak due to structural ageing. With economic or functional depreciation, the loss is usually calculated as a lump-sum deduction at the time that it occurs. In the case of physical depreciation, you usually spread it over the life of the improvement. Depreciation can only affect the improvements, not the land.

Measuring Depreciation

There are different ways of calculating the amount of depreciation as permitted by the Internal Revenue Code. Remember that depreciation is only deductible on the improvements. I disagree with that ruling, but the government hasn't seen fit to consult me on the question. In any case, there are several ways to figure out the amount of depreciation you may deduct from the income of a property.

Straight Line Method

One way is the "straight line method" of depreciation. Under this method, you must do two things to calculate the amount of depreciation you'll take in any given year. First, you decide how long the economic life of this improvement is. How long can the property be used for the purpose for which it was intended. Suppose you say a building has a useful economic life of 50 years; that doesn't mean that at the end of 50 years it might not still be standing. It means that, at the end of 50 years in this particular area, it will not be saleable or useable. There are tables suggesting useful life for various types of buildings. However, that means that every property has a specific useful life. Each taxpayer must be able to support his position on the useful life of his building with some reasonable facts. For example, you can show what the useful life is of other buildings in the area.

The useful economic life of the improvement is the first thing you decide. Then, you decide what the value of the building is new, less its salvage value. Suppose you decide that the economic life of the building is 25 years. Then, suppose you decide that the improvements (not the land) are worth $40,000 and that there is no salvage value. Under the straight line method, you simply divide the $40,000 by the 25 years, which will give you $1,600. So that means that you may take $1,600 per year, each and every year, for 25 years. With the straight line method, you take the same amount of depreciation each year.

If you wanted to think of this in terms of a percentage, you just divide the 25 years into 100%. One hundred per cent represents the total value of the new property. Divide it by 25 years, and that would give you 4% each year. It is the same thing, because 4% of $40,000 is $1,600.

Declining Balance Method

The next approach is the "declining balance method." There are two types of declining balance approaches. The easiest one is called the "double declining balance" or the "200% declining balance." The other approach is the 1½ or "150% declining balance." It will become self-explanatory if you understand this double declining balance method. This approach requires you to figure out what the straight line depreciation of the property would be and what your deduction would be per year—then double it.

Use the same example: $40,000 value with 25 years life equals $1,600 depreciation per year. In this case, you're allowed to double it, so you could deduct $3,200 the first year. The second year you do the same thing; you figure out the straight line depreciation. However, this time you have 24 years left and you must deduct from the $40,000 original value what has already been taken off as depreciation. This figure is now not $40,000 but $36,800. Related in percentages, this would be 8% the first year. A straight line of 4% times two is 8%. The second year it would be a little bit less. The second year it is 7.36%. The next year it is 6.77%, and so on. It is the tenth year before you deduct *less* than you would under the straight line method. The straight line method in the tenth year has you still deducting 4% per year. In the tenth year under the double declining balance, you're only deducting 3.78%.

Under the 1½ or 150% declining balance, you do the same thing except only at 1½ times or 150% of the straight line method instead of twice or 200%. These, along with the next method, are what is called an "accelerated method of depreciation." You are able to write off the cost of the improvement faster in its early years of life. You don't really have to understand how these are computed or how to compute them yourself, because you can get the tables with the information. Some people consider the 150% and the 200% as two different methods. However, I consider them to be one method with two variances.

Sum of the Years' Digits

The third method is the "sum of the years' digits." Again, you can refer to the table to get this figure, but here is how it is calculated: Use a fraction instead of a percentage (you can convert it to a percentage if you want to, obviously). The denominator of this fraction is the sum of the years' digits. The numerator is the years of life left in the improvement. If you're talking about the example with the 25-year life, the digits of the 25 years are 1, 2, 3, 4, and so on to 25. To calculate the denominator, therefore, you would add 1 plus 2 plus 3 plus 4, etc. You get 325 as the denominator. The first year you have the full 25 years of life left, so your numerator is 25. You may deduct 25/325ths (or 1/13th) of the value of the improvement.

A fast way to figure the sum of the years' digits (the denominator) is this: Multiply the number of separate numbers by the median (or middle) number. For example: $1 + 2 + 3 + 4 + 5$. There are five separate numbers and the middle one is 3. So, $1 + 2 + 3 + 4 + 5 = 15$ and so does 5×3. Or, consider: $1 + 2 + 3 + 4 + 5 + 6 + 7 + 8 + 9 + 10$. There are ten separate numbers and the middle point is halfway between 5 and 6 or 5.5. Therefore, you multiply 5.5 by 10 and get 55. Or, to use the 25 years in the previous example: $1 + 2 + 3 + 4 + 5 + 6 + 7 + 8 + 9 + 10 + 11 + 12 + 13 + 14 + 15 + 16 + 17 + 18 + 19 + 20 + 21 + 22 + 23 + 24 + 25$. There are 25 separate numbers and the middle point is 13. Hence, $25 \times 13 = 325$.

Some Other Aspects

Let's talk about a couple of other things in connection with depreciation.

Salvage Value

We mentioned salvage value. The salvage value is whatever the value of the property is at the end of its useful life. Take the case of a $40,000 improvement. You may not use the $40,000 as the basis of depreciation, if at the end of its useful life you could salvage $2,000 out of it. You would have to use $38,000 as the basis of its value, and depreciate the $38,000. However, when you're trying to figure out what the salvage value is of an improvement 25 years from now, you're really "crystal balling," that is, guessing. As a matter of practice, most people write it off and say there is no salvage value.

In fact, it is often the case that there is not only no salvage value, but it costs money to tear the improvement down. If you wanted to get real technical, you could say that, since it will cost $1,000 to tear the improvement down, you want to depreciate it on a $41,000 basis. Unfortunately, I doubt that Internal Revenue would permit that. So, as far as salvage value is concerned, you will usually just write it off as zero.

Accelerated Methods

We have talked about the straight line method, the two kinds of declining balance, and the sum of the years' digits. There is a limit as to who may use these methods. Anyone may use the straight line method. However, in the case of the 200% or double declining balance method and the sum of the years' digits method, only the first user of that property for income purposes may use them.

If the builder constructs an apartment building, begins to rent the apartments, collects rent, and then sells it to you, you are not the first user—he is. Therefore, you cannot use the sum of the year's digits or the 200% declining balance. You may use the 150% declining balance method, and you can always use the straight line method.

Furthermore, once you are committed to one method of depreciation on the property, you cannot change methods without permission from Internal Revenue. Except that you may convert from an accelerated method to the straight line method, provided that it doesn't result in your getting a bigger annual deduction. Remember the example used concerning the 25-year life with the 200% declining balance as opposed to the straight line method? You got 4% a year using the straight line method, or you got from 8% down for the first nine years using the 200% declining balance method. With the double declining balance you get more than 4% per year in those first nine years. However, in the tenth year under double declining balance, you drop below 4% (actually to 3.78%). At that point, you cannot shift to the straight line method because you'd be getting an increase in depreciation. However, you could have shifted in a year prior to that.

Selection of Method

When you become the owner of a piece of property, you may elect to use any depreciation method that you would normally be permitted to use, regardless of what method was used by the prior owner. The prior owner might have started with a double declining balance as the first user. You may decide that you can do better with some other method, perhaps the 150% declining balance. You may keep the property for eight or ten years and then sell it. The third buyer may use the straight line method. You must also remember that the basis of your depreciation is the value of the *improvement*, not the total property.

Some investors will buy a new property which makes them the first user. However, you can be the first user of a very old property. Suppose you owned a single-family home for 20 years, and then you bought a new home. If you decide not to sell your old house but, instead, keep it as a rental property, you may be the first user of *income* from that property. Many professional investors take an income property as a first user and keep it for seven or eight years. Then they sell it and move on to something else. Or, they may keep control of the property by selling to another entity they control. They may have originally taken title in their own name as an individual, then they turn around and sell it to a corporation which they own.

Land-Improvement Ratio

You may know the value of the total property, but how does it split between improvements and land? This is important since only the improvements can be depreciated for income tax purposes. The value of the land is supposed to be reasonable. You can establish it, but you always run the risk of having Internal Revenue say your split or ratio is wrong. If the value of the land is really different than what you said it was on your tax return, you've taken too much depreciation. So you may owe some back taxes. One way to confirm what the split is would be to get a professional appraiser to value the land and improvements. Another conventional approach which is commonly used is the apportionment of value between land and building that the tax assessor uses. If you go down to the tax office and look up your property, you will see that there are three values given: a value for land, a value for improvements, and a value of the total of the two. So if it turns out that the value for the two is assessed at $100,000, $40,000 of which is land and $60,000 of which is improvements, then most people take the position that 40% is the price they paid for it and 60% is improvements.

Is an Accelerated Method Right for You?

Many people assume that the ideal situation is to take accelerated depreciation if you can. This is not necessarily true, because when you sell the property for a gain, your profit is *not* the difference between what you paid for it and what you get for it. It is the difference between the *depreciated value* on your books and the sale price you get. Depreciation is entirely, not "tax-free income." Depreciation allows you to take a portion of the income on the property and convert it to a capital gains profit. This has the advantage of allowing you to pay a smaller tax then you would normally pay on ordinary income. So, there is a portion that is tax free, but it is not all tax free. For example, if you write off $10,000 in the first eight years by way of depreciation and then sell, you must pay tax on the $10,000.

The increase in value of the property may have been only in the land. Since the land is not the basis of your depreciation, you may think you are ahead of the game—but you're not. This is because you can only depreciate the improvement—this value. If you bought a property for $40,000, wrote off $10,000 in depreciation, then sold it for $60,000, you've made $30,000 profit—taxable profit.

Demolition

Can you demolish the improvement and write that off in the year you do it? Normally, if you bought the property with the intentions of demolishing the improvement, you must capitalize the cost of the improvement. That is, you must take the demolition cost and add that to the cost of the new building. Then, you spread it out over the life of the new building.

If you erect a new building that is going to last 25 years, you've got to spread out the demolition cost over 25 years. Suppose it cost you $5,-000 to demolish the old improvements. You have to spread that $5,000 over the 25-year life of the new building. This is because you bought the property with the intention of demolishing the existing building. The demolition was voluntary on your part.

On the other hand, you may not buy a property with the intention of demolishing the improvements. Suppose it is a home you've lived in for many years and you've decided to redevelop it with an apartment house. You have to demolish the old house to do it. In that case, you may charge off the entire cost of demolitions that year. This is an important factor for many people to consider. Also, when a governmental agency condemns the property as being unfit for use and directs you to demolish it, that is a case of involuntary demolition. You can write off the entire cost in the year that you incur it.

Repairs vs. Capital Improvements

Every time you spend something on a property, you are faced with the question of whether it is a repair, maintenance, operating expense, or capital improvement. If it is a capital improvement, you have to spread the cost over the remaining years of life of that building. If it is an operating cost like property management, taxes, utility expenses, or insurance premiums, then you can charge that off in the year that you pay it. Most people want to charge off as much as they can in the year that the operating charge is paid for obvious reasons.

Sometimes, it is difficult to determine whether it is an expense, a repair, or a capital improvement. Generally, the position is that, if it adds useful life to the building or it results in additional income by remodeling and creating a new type of building, it is a capital improvement. This must be amortized over the life of the building. If, on the other hand, it is something required to keep the building in good repair— fit for occupancy, for the comfort, convenience, or safety of the tenants— it is probably a repair.

Taxes, Interest, and Carrying Charges

On investment property, you can decide whether you want to capitalize or charge off the taxes, interest, and carrying charges. If you buy 10 acres of land on speculation, you may either deduct the taxes, the interest, and other carrying charges of holding that land each year as you incur them, or you can simply accumulate them. If you let them accumulate, your cost basis is much higher when you sell the property. Thus, your taxable profit is much lower. That may sound odd because many people want to deduct as much as they can each year. However, suppose you're in a situation where you are now in a low income tax bracket. And, suppose, that in five years when you plan to sell this land, you expect to be in a very high income tax bracket. In that case, you want to defer as many deductions as possible until the later date. You are, therefore, not too interested in deductions right now.

Soil and Water Conservation

Conservation is in the public interest, so money you spend for soil or water conservation on your property is fully deductible in the year that you incur it. Suppose you decide to conserve the soil of a particular property by planting ground-cover or channelizing a creek that goes through the property. That is fully deductible because the government encourages this.

POINTS TO KEEP IN MIND

- *Depreciation is a loss in value that may be due to either physical, functional, or economic causes.*

- *Among the methods of measuring the amount of depreciation are these:*

  –Straight line.
  –Declining balance.
  –Sum of the years' digits.

- *Some other aspects of tax deductions to remember are:*

  –Salvage value.
  –Land-improvement ratio.
  –Demolition.
  –Repairs vs. capital improvement.
  –Taxes, interest, and carrying charges.
  –Soil and water conservation.

VII

OPERATING
REAL ESTATE

···20···

Landlord's
Lease Checklist

When you enter into a lease as a landlord, there are many *business* considerations that you must keep in mind. Unfortunately, too many landlords rely entirely on their attorneys or a stock (printed lease they bought at the drugstore for 50 cents to protect their *business* interests). The problem is that too many attorneys understand too little about business and drugstore leases, which supposedly fit *all* situations but usually don't fit any.

So, I have set forth in the material that follows some of the things that you —as a landlord—should consider from a business point of view. This is not legal advice. It is business advice. It is designed to protect your business interests.

Not all of what follows will apply to all leasing circumstances. However, a great many of the items and considerations mentioned are valid under most conditions. In some instances, the comments are made from both the landlord's and the tenant's angle so that you can understand what may be the objections from the other side of the desk.

1. **Lessor and Lessee.** Obviously, if you are the landlord you don't have to worry about *you* because you know you're honest. If you are a tenant, however, you may want to make sure that the person who signs the lease is the landlord, not the landlord's son or a front corporation that has no right to lease the property. Suppose you were to lease a property from somebody and it was owned by the XYZ Corporation. You are at worst a trespasser and at best a squatter. If you're the landlord, the same thing applies to the tenant. Make sure that the person who signs the lease is the person who has the right to sign it. The authority to sign, if he represents a corporation, must obtain corporate resolution and the corporate seal. Know that this is the person who signed the lease. This is very important because we're in a very strong era of franchising. A representative of some large franchise company may come to you and say, "Look, here's our statement. We're worth $3 million and we want to lease this corner to put up a fried clam stand." You say that sounds marvelous, and grant them a 15-year lease. So they draw up the lease and it is signed by the Fried Clam Corporation #342 of Reseda. When you investigate, it has total assets of 12 cents and a book of blue chip stamps. You find out that it is a separate corporation; it has nothing to do with the mother corporation. Or, the lease may be signed by a franchisee; he goes broke; and the franchise company is only interested in selling him clams in exchange for clams of a different kind—that's how they make their money. For example, a franchiser sells Coke to all its franchisees. You and I could go down and buy a case of 24 bottles of Coca Cola for $2.40. A franchiser sells them to the franchisees for $6.25. This is how franchisers make their money.

2. **Premises.** Are the premises that are being leased identified? Make sure you clearly explain exactly what it is you're leasing the man. He may think because you happen to have a building in the middle of 2 acres of asphalt that he is leasing a store plus the 2 acres of asphalt on which to park. You may be planning on putting a chicken plucking factory on that 2 acres of asphalt, leaving him no parking. So make sure you clearly state what you're leasing, not just the physical facility in terms of the improvements, but also the parking and all the other things.

3. **Terms.** The term of the lease is fairly simple. Suppose a 15-year lease starts in 1965 and will expire in 1980. There's no problem unless you've

got to build for a tenant, or remodel, or something like that. The law says you cannot legally enter into a contract which cannot be fulfilled within 99 years, or in the cases of probates 99 years plus 21. Nevertheless, the law says you must have an absolute starting date in order for the lease to be valid. You cannot say that you'll lease me this store or this apartment when it is finished, when it is remodeled, or when construction is completed because that is a very indefinite thing. This is an absurd example, but suppose something happens that delays completion of the construction for 90 years, then a 15-year lease is illegal because it goes beyond 99 years from the time you first enter into it. You must pick an absolute starting date. The usual procedure is that the lease will start when you take possession of the property or on the first of January, whichever occurs first, but in no case later than July 15. You have that leeway in case of a strike or shortage of materials.

4. **Consider Rental.** What does the man pay for his rent? What is included in the rent, and what is not included? I'm going to pay you $300 a month—what am I going to get for it? Are you going to include paying the utilities or are you going to pay the repair and maintenance? Are you going to take care of the common areas like the parking lot and the walkways, collecting the rubbish? What is included in the rent? Usually what the man pays on a store or an apartment involves a lot more than just "X" dollars and a month to live in this space or to do business in it. It involves so many dollars a month to do business in the store *plus* a proportionate share of taking care of the parking lot, a proportionate share of the tax increases, and a proportionate share of utilities. Make sure that everybody is clear on what the rental is. A lease for an apartment is worthless from the point of view of the landlord, but there should be some written agreement, even a month-to-month written agreement, which simply sets forth what the rent will be, who pays what, who pays the utilities, who takes care of the yard, and who picks up the rubbish. The reason the lease is no good is because of the many problems you get involved with. One of the things I don't like about leases is they keep me as a landlord from raising the rent. But, it doesn't keep a tenant from moving out on me, does it? If you go off to Las Vegas spending what you think is next month's rent money, you come back and half your building is empty—they all moved out Saturday and Sunday. What are you going to do? Do you have to hire somebody to find them?

5. **Inflation Protection.** All landlords on commercial property or industrial property that sign a 15-year or longer lease are concerned because of inflation. Inflation keeps eating away the purchasing power of the rent they are going to receive, and they try to evolve some method of getting more money as inflation keeps going up while the pur-

chasing power keeps going down. There are many ways to do this. One is to tie the rent to the cost of living index that is published by some governmental agency, and another is to base it on a percentage of the value of the property. On net ground leases this is common. If you were to rent or lease a piece of ground for whatever—a gas station, an office building, etc.—and you agree to pay 7% of the fair value of the property (it is a 25-, or 35-, or 55-year lease), what will generally happen is you will say you'll pay 7% of the value of the property each year and start out by agreeing that the value of the property the first year or whatever period of time is $100,000. At the end of five years, you get together and try to agree on what the value is at the time to set the rent for the next five years. If you can't agree, then you will each appoint an appraiser, the two appraisers will appoint a third appraiser, and you'll both be bound by the decision of the majority of these three appraisers as to what the value is. In retail leases the most common device is the so-called percentage lease, where you say you will pay me $6,000 a year or 5% of your gross sales, whichever is greater. If your gross sales are $200,000, 5% of $200,000 would be $10,000, that means $10,000 (4% is more than $6,000/year) you'll be paying me because it is more than the minimum guarantee. There are all kinds of questions that come up with the percentage lease. In the trade the percentage lease is known as an invitation to steal, because the first question that you put in a lease asks what is included in gross sales—everything? The tenant will say absolutely not because he has, for example, gum ball machines, cigarette machines, telephones, stamp machines, all sorts of coin-operated machines on the premises. They are just convenience devices to bring people into the store. He'll lose money on those, so he isn't going to pay you on that. He'll also lose money on tobacco, so he isn't going to pay you on tobacco. What about merchandise that is returned for refund? He has to get credit for that, and so on. You can go on and on with all sorts of problems. For example, how, after you decide what is included in gross sales, do you prove what the gross sales are? You could stand at the cash register with a little notebook all day and write them down. Most people simply say, you just take the cash register tapes. How many times have you been in a store where they've rung up a sale and made change for two more out of the drawer without ringing the two up? The best method that is commonly used is to take the certified franchise tax returns that are filed with the state for the basis of determining sales tax. If the tenant lies on those it is a felony, so he is less likely to lie. Suppose you suspect he is cheating and you want an audit made of his books. Who pays for the audit? If he is cheating you, normally he pays. If you find out that he isn't cheating you, then usually the landlord pays. You allow the man generally some kind of a leeway like one-tenth of 1% or half of 1%, give or take some. How frequently are the gross sales computed? They are computed monthly, quarterly, semiannually, or annually. The landlord wants them computed hourly. The tenant wants them computed once in a decade because usually you'll argue about whether it will be quarterly or annually. The tenant wants it annually because his good months will be offset by his bad months. If he loses money—suppose he makes $200,000 in gross sales in a year—but you're computing this annually, then you just average out his good months with his bad months. If he has four months where he has to make $500 a month (his guaranteed minimum) he has to make at 5% $10,000 a month just to meet his guaranteed minimum. Let's say in four months he makes only $4,000 and the other eight months he makes $184,000. Those four months, if you're computing it annually, will help to offset the good months. If you're computing it monthly, he will have to pay you the $500 each of those four months that he is below his minimum on the sales. He'll still have to pay you the average on the big months. That is why a tenant likes to have the audit done annually.

6. **Taxes.** Who pays the taxes? Commonly the landlord pays the taxes the first year, and the tenant pays all increases over that. Suppose the landlord defaults and doesn't pay the taxes. The tenant, who may have made a big investment in this property, stands in jeopardy of the property being sold for taxes and losing his position as the tenant. So, frequently, a smart tenant will say if the landlord doesn't pay the taxes he is supposed to pay, the tenant may pay them for him, resulting in a credit against the rent.

7. **Repair and Maintenance.** Who pays for what repairs? Normally in a commercial building the landlord takes care of exterior walls and the roof only, and the tenant takes care of everything else. In a residential building or apartment house, normally the landlord takes care of everything unless it is the tenant's negligence.

8. **Insurance.** In a commercial or industrial building, you will want the tenant to carry a certain amount of insurance which names you, the landlord, as a co-insured. It doesn't cost any more premium. If somebody slips on a banana peel outside of the store, they will sue everybody in sight. That's just standard practice. They're going to sue the landlord as well as the tenant. The tenant's insurance, for which he has already paid the premium, should also cover the landlord. In view of the constantly rising size of awards, this insurance should be pretty high. Depending on the property, I would say it should be like $100,000 to $300,000 in today's market. If you slip and break your little finger and go to a jury, they may give you $75,000. Also, the landlord should have the right to approve the insurance company

with which the insurance is carried. If it is the Montecash Insurance Company of Casablanca, you might be a little bit nervous about their ability to pay off. Insurance companies have failed.

9. **Liens.** You should also have protection against liens. If the tenant makes improvements on the property and doesn't pay for them, you know who the laborers and the material suppliers go after. They lien your property, and you as the landlord are legally responsible. So you should have a provision protecting you against liens in the lease, in addition to which you should require that the tenant gives you at least 30 days notice before he starts construction. When he does start construction, put a big notice up called a "notice of nonresponsibility." It is a notice to everybody that does work on the job or delivers material on the job, that you, the landlord, are not responsible for any on-the-job accidents. You should also record a copy of that notice of nonresponsibility.

10. **New Construction.** I mentioned previously some of the problems of new construction in terms of the starting date of the lease. If there is new construction to be done, you had better get a "completion bond" to make sure that the work is finished. There is nothing quite as sickening as signing a 25-year lease with somebody who says he will lease the ground from you and that he isn't going to put up an office building, and then going out there one day to find that he is putting up a five-story office building. The building is up in the shell with no windows or siding when all of a sudden construction stops. What happened? The contractor went broke. The tenant can't get another contractor because he hasn't got the money. He paid the contractor so much money in advance to keep him going that he just went broke. He's real sorry about the lease. He'll just have to hand the building over to you. If you're having the building built yourself by a contractor, a completion bond isn't a bad idea.

11. **Security Money.** Tenants always scream about security money. A man comes in to lease something from you, a store or apartment—you say that you'll lease it to him but you want the first month's rent in advance plus the equivalent of three months' rent as security. If he moves out or leaves the place dirty, you'll have a chance to clean it up and recoup some of your money. You get into all sorts of arguments about this. If it is a ten-year lease with the security money representing the last three months, the man will say he's giving you $500 a month. So if you want him to put up $1,500 with you as security for ten years, you should pay him 4.8%. Why should he lose that interest? You're going to have to do it if you want the space. You could put it in a joint savings account.

12. **Destruction.** All leases also provide for the case of destruction of property. In the event of a fire, you will be lucky if the place burns

to the ground. Otherwise, you're stuck with a building that is one-quarter burned and an expense to clean up. The problems arise when it doesn't burn down completely or it isn't totally damaged. If it is damaged or destroyed completely, the tenant says that the lease is off. If you rebuild it, it will take six months. During those six months there'll be no rent, but when it is ready he can go in and start business again. Suppose there is a 20-year lease and the man is occupying a 25,000-square foot reinforced concrete building with a supermarket in it. Six months before the end of the lease, an earthquake knocks the building down or partially down. Under the terms just cited, you are obligated to reconstruct that building for the six months left on the lease. Normally, the landlord is given the option to either rebuild or not. If he doesn't start within a reasonable time like 60 to 90 days, the tenant can say the lease is cancelled as of this time. That is fair and equitable. Another problem arises when only 5% of the premises are destroyed, but the 5% that is destroyed make it impossible for the man to do business in the other 95%. That is a problem that should be dealt with in the lease. The front of the store has collapsed or burned down; you can't get into the place. The same thing is true of condemnation which was covered briefly before.

13. **Re-entry.** When the landlord leases the premises, he does not legally have the right to go back on the property without the permission of the tenant, as long as the tenant is not in default. If the tenant pays his rent, lives up to his obligations, and the landlord comes on the premises without permission of the tenant, the tenant can throw him off because during the period of that lease the landlord has no right to enter the premises. But the landlord *should* have the right. So, generally, a clause is put in the lease giving the landlord the right to enter the premises at reasonable periods of time for the purpose of inspecting it or doing any repair work that is his responsibility.

14. **Grace.** Normally, in most leases we get involved in, we provide for what is called a grace period when we say that neither the landlord nor the tenant are in default of the lease until ten to 30 days after the other party has notified them in writing that they are in default. You might be in default of the lease as a landlord and not know about it. If you're off on vacation and you haven't done something which is supposed to happen under the terms of the lease, the tenant says you're in default as of this minute. If you're given ten days time or 30 days time after you receive a written notification from the tenant, then you have a chance to correct it.

15. **Assignment and Subletting.** If a lease is assigned, it means that the original tenant is off the hook and a new tenant is taking over his position. When it is a sublet, the original tenant is leasing it to another tenant but the original tenant is still on the lease. Most landlords will not permit the assignment or subletting of the property without their

written permission. The reason for this is, you may lease the property originally to Safeway Stores, etc.; they decide they can't make it in that location, so they want out. They assign the lease to FM Discount Store, and the question of stability comes in again. You are on the hook for this new tenant unless you have the right to approve them.

16. **Condemnation.** This clause works much like the one on destruction. If a party takes all the property, there is no problem. But suppose he just takes a little slice across the driveway so nobody can get into the parking lot? The tenant can't do business.

17. **Options.** I despise options from the point of view of the landlord. They are a one-way street. They tie the landlord down but not the tenant. The tenant has the option to renew for ten years. What does that do? That ties the landlord down. You have to do something; he doesn't. Generally, you should give him a weasel word in there, saying that you'll give him an option and the right of first refusal. This means that if his lease is up next month and you have another tenant who will pay three times as much rent, he has the right of first refusal.

18. **Signs.** It is very important to have sign control. Don't let tenants put up signs that are not in keeping with the kind of building you're trying to run there. You should not permit a tenant to put up signs or decorations without your written permission.

19. **Co-tenancy.** Sometimes a tenant will insist that his lease should not start until another tenant moves in. For example, let's say your tenant is a dry cleaner. You have a little shopping center, and you've got a supermarket scheduled for this store. A man comes along and says he wants the store right next door for a dry cleaning place. He is going to starve in this dry cleaning store unless the market is also there and open. If the market goes out, again using Safeway Stores as an example, he has the right to terminate.

20. **Zoning.** You need a clause about zoning because zoning laws and building ordinances limit the kinds of uses to which buildings can be put. If you're the landlord, one of the things you should be sure to include in your lease is that the tenant has investigated the zoning ordinances and the building regulations for the use of this building, and that he assumes responsibility that his use of the building he is renting is legal. If the building is in a C-2 zone, then certain types of activities are permitted there. If it is a C-1 zone, certain other types are permitted and many types of uses are *not* permitted. In addition to the zone, there is an occupancy code which is part of the Building and Safety Code. It permits certain types of occupancies. The Building Department makes requirements for a certain amount of exits, certain kinds of floor coverings, or all sorts of things that have to be done for different kinds of uses. You may be in a C-2 zone which permits a restaurant. But there may not be an occupancy permit for a

restaurant in this particular building. If you lease it to a restaurant then you might be in trouble, because you have to make certain changes in the building at your expense to make it suitable for occupancy by a restaurant. In the case of a restaurant for instance, the floor covering cannot be asphalt tile which is all right for a shoe store or almost any other retail operation. The floor must have vinyl tile because of the food problem; there is going to be spillage on the floor. They don't want the food and grease to soak into the floor. In addition to that, there has to be certain floor drains or sinks so that the floor may actually be washed down, and the water will drain into the floor. There has to be certain extra fire protections because of a very high fire hazard with restaurants. You may be required to put these in. For a shoestore one rest room is sufficient, but for any kind of eating establishment or a bar you must have two rest rooms. Each rest room must have two doors between the inner part of the rest room and the bar or the restaurant. So you may have to put in an extra foyer to the rest rooms. This is expensive. Once the tenant has investigated all the ordinances and codes, and is satisfied that this building is suitable for him to occupy, he then assumes all liability.

21. **Parking.** You should always determine who gets what parking or if it is mutual parking. The tenant's problem will depend on what kind of businesses are next to him. A doctor's office will need an extensive parking lot; those people will be waiting a long time. Perhaps the first tenant has a business that requires several available parking spaces to be available at one time. His customers come and go. It would hurt his business if the patients of his neighbor, the doctor, were parking in his spaces. If the tenant is given the exclusive right to use six parking spaces, and a customer of someone else parks there, then the tenant can do a variety of things. But the question of what is to be done by whom revolves around not just who is taking care of the parking lot, but who is enforcing the rules. If the landlord is enforcing the rules, then he has the responsibility of keeping those stalls clear, if it is called for in the lease. If not, then if he doesn't do it, the tenant probably has grounds to reduce his rent. Now, if the tenant is the one who has to take care of the parking lot, then he has to police it. In addition to getting the exclusive right to park in a couple of stalls, there should be some indication of who is going to patrol and be responsible for policing. There are a variety of ways of doing that —complaining to the other tenants is not too effective. Signs that have a very specific warning are more effective than the usual municipal code violation signs. The specific warning signs may not be legal, but they are effective psychologically.

22. **Fixtures.** Fixtures are usually those things which are permanently attached to the property; they become part of the real property. In business there are certain things known as trade fixtures which cus-

tomarily belong to the tenant, no matter how they are attached to the premises. Included are showcases, shelving, usually the lights if the tenant provided them. Those appliances and fixtures that are used in the normal trade of the business, no matter how they are affixed, are usually removable. That is, they are removable with the provision that any damage to the property caused by the removal of these fixtures must be repaired by the tenant. Another point on the negative side, from the point of view of the landlord, is that you should require certain fixtures be removed if you don't want them. It is not unusual for a tenant to put in partitioning and build improvements onto the property. You may want him to leave the improvements behind when he departs; this is all right. However, suppose you lease to a gasoline station. The gas station has to have large tanks underground. If the tanks are old, it is not worth the effort to dig them up. They are going to want to leave them buried there. The reason you care is that unless you are going to rent to another tenant that is in the same business, the Fire Dept. requires that you fill those tanks with cement or take them out of the ground. Either way it is expensive. Suppose you rent to a savings and loan association, a jeweler, or a banker. They put in a vault which has 18-inch thick, reinforced concrete walls. Your next tenant complains that he doesn't have enough sales space. He will want you to remove the vault. It doesn't come out easy when it is 18 inches thick. It will cost a lot of money to take it out. You may want to require that the bank or jewelry store remove it.

23. **Laws.** You should require that the tenant conform to and obey all laws and city ordinances that are now in force or may be passed in the future concerning his premises. Suppose they pass a law in the future that requires a specific type of electrical fixture or sprinkler system. Who will pay for it? You should require that the tenant comply with all existing and future laws during the term of the lease.

24. **Lessee Improvements.** Provide that all improvements made which you want are to remain with the property. This is a cheap way to improve your property. The tenant will say he wants to have the property air conditioned. You make a deal to reduce the cost of the rent proportionately with the cost of the air conditioning, if the tenant will pay for the air conditioning. This has tax advantages.

25. **Condition of Premises.** The tenant should accept the premises as is, or specify what is to be changed. There should be no verbal understanding if you're going to repaint, refloor, reroof, or air-condition.

26. **Waiver of Breach.** Sometimes a tenant will have difficulty in making his rent payment on time. There is a fairly standard type of clause, that any attorney will require or any printed lease will have, called a "waiver of breach clause." It simply says that if you agree to waive, to

forget about some breach of the lease for the tenant at some given time, this does not mean that you agree to waive all future breaches. The waiver of breach allows the tenant to pay his rent later only for this month. It doesn't mean that his rent payment date is automatically shifted in the following months.

27. **Attorneys' Fees.** Most landlords' leases call for a clause concerning attorneys' fees. If the landlord sues the tenant, then the tenant will pay the attorney's fees of the landlord, whether the landlord wins, loses, or draws. That is a landlord's lease. A reasonably intelligent tenant will have some negative reaction to that because it gives the landlord the right to sue him on anything at any time. It is going to be the tenant's expense, so usually if either party sues the other party, whoever loses pays the other's attorney's fees. This only concerns itself when the case is settled in court. You should make some provision for settling out of court. If the suit is settled out of court, the person who offers the settlement or decides to settle should be obligated for the attorneys' fees—both attorneys' fees.

28. **Arbitration.** Attorneys dislike the "arbitration clause." I think this is very good to have because it takes so long to be scheduled in court. In the meantime, you may be losing money. You may win the case, but the time element is very crucial. I generally call for an arbitration clause which says that if there is any argument about any point in the lease, each side will appoint an arbitrator. The two arbitrators will appoint a third arbitrator, and they will arbitrate the dispute. Both sides will agree to be bound by the majority vote of these three arbitrators. You'll share the cost of arbitration 50-50. In that way you can settle a dispute in a matter of 30 days, instead of waiting perhaps two years. The arbitrator has to be somebody who is mutually acceptable to both landlord and tenant.

29. **Quiet Possession.** The tenant will usually demand "quiet possession." This is another standard term in law which means that the landlord is obligated to protect the tenant from the claims of any other person who says that *he* is the tenant in that place. You might encounter this sort of situation: You lease to Joe Doaks for ten years; after a year, Joe Doaks abandons the property. You wait for awhile, then you take possession of the property under the abandonment clause of your lease. You release it to another tenant. After a year, Joe Doaks comes back. He sees that the present tenant is doing well and business conditions have improved. So Joe Doaks insists that the present tenant has illegal possession because Doaks has possibly ten years left on his lease. He further contends that he can make an average of $10,000 profit a year; therefore, he sues you for $130,000 because you've deprived him of that profit. Your normal obligation as a landlord is to protect the tenant against that kind of a claim.

30. **Waste.** This term simply means that while every tenant has the right to make fair use of the property, he cannot wantonly destroy it or purposely allow it to deteriorate. He is the tenant and has the exclusive right of using the property, but that doesn't mean he can take an axe and chop up the walls. You will need a clause to take care of this.

31. **Heirs and Successors.** This says that the lease will be binding on the heirs and successors. This is important if the tenant dies or the tenant merges or assigns the lease.

32. **Holding Over.** Normally, you have a clause for holding over. It means the tenant can stay in the premises after the lease has expired with your permission. Usually, the clause about holding over says that if the tenant holds over after the lease has expired, he will hold over on the same terms and conditions on a month-to-month basis, rather than renewing the lease. He will pay the same rent as he paid the last month of the lease. If he has been paying $350 a month and the lease expires, he continues to pay $350. But, there is a catch. Sometimes as a tax device, landlords will try unsuccessfully to outsmart Internal Revenue. They might charge $300 a month, but they want the tenant to pay the first and last months' rent in advance. That is a total of $600. The tenant wants the landlord to pay interest if he wishes to hold the $600 for 15 years. The tenant says that the landlord is not only holding his money, but also technically he can't charge that off his income tax as rent until 15 years from now. The landlord may have to pay tax on it in the year he received it, unless he sets it aside in a special way as a security deposit. The landlord may utilize another method to avoid paying interest on the $600 and also allow the tenant to charge it off as an expense. This could be done by writing the lease up this way: Consider the rent on the first month to be $598; the rent on the last two months is going to be $1 each month. That way the landlord can write off the $598 right now. There could be a problem when he gets to the end of the lease and goes into the holding over period, however. The tenant could pay him each month the same rent as he paid the last month of the lease, which was $1 a month. That is a disadvantage of this arrangement. What usually is done in the holding over part of a percentage lease is either continue the percentage or the guaranteed minimum plus the percentage. If the landlord wishes to collect his rent on a flat basis (that is, where there is no percentage), then he says the tenant will pay the average monthly rental that he has paid over the last year of the lease, which would take into consideration any percentages that he would pay.

33. **Notice.** This is an important feature. Where are notices to be delivered? How do landlord and tenant get in touch with each other in terms of co-transactions? The lease normally contains addresses to which the notices may be delivered. It is not wise to have the notice

to the tenant delivered to the address of the store or the apartment. It is better to use some other address, like the tenant's home. If the tenant moves out, you can't deliver the notice to him. Technically, you can deliver the notice by tacking it on the wall or the front door. But, in order to be absolutely sure that he gets it, you'd like to have it reach him personally. You should specify when or what will be considered as delivering the notice. Does it have to be delivered to the party in person? As a process-server will tell you, it is not delivered until you actually touch the person. You may agree that a notice will be considered delivered when it is posted in the U.S. mail, addressed to his residence with the postage prepaid, or when it is handed to the person. If a notice has been effectively delivered when you deposit it in the mail or set it in transmission by Western Union, then you're not worried about that problem.

34. **Amendments.** Always include a statement to the effect that this lease is the total agreement. There are no other agreements or modifications that are not contained in the lease. Any changes that will be made in the lease in the future must be in writing and signed by both parties. Inevitably, the tenant is going to come to you and ask when you plan to finish the parking lot, etc. It may be that you mentioned you were going to work on the parking lot. It isn't in the lease, however. Be sure the lease is complete, with all parties concerned having a good understanding of the terms.

35. **Other Property.** The tenant may want to restrict you from leasing any other property you have in the neighborhood to a business that is competitive to his own. This would seem to be fairly legitimate, but it actually turns out to be a pain in the neck from the point of view of the landlord. It is customary in shopping centers to give exclusives. A man comes up and says he wants to open up a fish store, but he wants to be the only one there. You say you'll give him an exclusive. But suppose a man comes in with a shoe store and wants to be the only shoe store there. You'd better stop and think about that one for a minute. This man may sell a price line of shoes that doesn't meet the demands of the neighborhood. It wouldn't be good to limit the price category. You don't want to limit yourself to one shoe store. Suppose he wants to put in a family shoe store. It may not be adequate to serve the different age groups. The family shoe store would be too much of a limit. You would want other shoe stores that specialize in maybe men's or women's shoes exclusively.

36. **Rules and Regulations.** Normally a lease will contain a clause that permits the landlord to prepare or issue rules and regulations for the operation of the premises, which all tenants agree to abide by. That is open ended because the rules will change from time to time, but they are designed primarily to make it possible for everybody to live

in the place comfortably. For example, some of the rules you'd use for an office building is that you would not permit tenants to use heavy-load electrical equipment without permission (this is to avoid power overloading on building service); keeping of animals, flammable materials, poisonous or noxious materials should be forbidden; loud singing, whistling, or playing of musical instruments, radios, or television sets should be forbidden; no use of elevators to move furniture or equipment except when permitted; and, no placement of heavy furniture or equipment without permission of landlord so as to avoid overloading floor sections.

POINTS TO KEEP IN MIND

The landlord's lease checklist is a guide to business aspects of leasing real property.

- *Identify the lessor and lessee.*
- *Identify the premises to be leased, including parking.*
- *Set forth the term of the lease.*
- *Set out the rent and all other payments to be made.*
- *Clarify who handles repairs, maintenance, and construction.*
- *Be sure of insurance coverage.*
- *What happens in event of liens, condemnation, or destruction?*
- *Security money—whose possession and how much?*
- *Should there be a grace period?*
- *Terms of re-entry, default, subletting, and assignment.*
- *Are co-tenants required by tenant?*
- *Options, zoning, and sign control.*
- *Who owns fixtures and tenant improvements?*
- *Possession, waivers, and legal fees.*
- *Waste, holding over, and arbitration.*
- *Notice, amendments, and other property.*
- *Rules and regulations.*

INDEX